How to win at Handicap Racing

by
Patrick Kilgallon

ISBN: 0900611 51 0

**RACEFORM LTD.,
COMPTON, NEWBURY, BERKSHIRE RG16 0NL**

Printed in Great Britain by David Green Printers Ltd, Kettering, Northamptonshire

FOREWORD

by Tony Stafford

Racing Editor, Daily Telegraph

Many years ago, I was asked to write a booklet on winner-finding. I found the exercise rewarding in that it gave me the chance to distill my opinions and thoughts into a logical order.

In writing this Foreword to Patrick Kilgallon's book, the same feeling of renewed awareness shone through, and his work reminds us all that there are profits to be made from backing horses.

Handicaps and their solution have long been an abiding passion of my own. Patrick Kilgallon's own betting seems to have been conducted in a much more disciplined way than mine, but his essential message is similarly based.

The disciplines he advocates are sound indeed. Value bets, fewer rather than more often, in decent-class races generally on good tracks would sum up one of his themes.

Racing in Britain does indeed have a seasonal rhythm which all-weather winter Flat racing—if confined as at present to non-entities—cannot alter. Mr Kilgallon uses that rhythm to identify suitable handicap opportunities.

I particularly like his ideas on the minimum prices to be accepted in any race. Short-priced losers are the surest way, as he says, "to Carey Street". Bankruptcy and racing involvement have been uneasy but regular bedfellows since the sport began. This book will lessen the risk that any of its readers could go that way.

After more than 20 years attempting to put readers on to the occasional winner which their own granny could not have found herself, I concur with Mr Kilgallon's view that serious form study is the only answer.

In these days of abundant television broadcast of races in betting shops, the ability to assess form rather than blindly accept the views of others is more vital than ever.

The serious mistake early in a jump race is one example where the careful betting shop viewer can enjoy an advantage. Mr Kilgallon ignores jumping in this book, because, as he says, mistakes alter the calculations. But his message is still a forceful one for Flat-race purposes.

Finally, for nothing else, I would read and re-read this book to remind me that any betting I do should be carefully monitored.

Expenses to and from the races mount up and small wins are soon swallowed up. It seems Mr Kilgallon makes it pay. Following his ideas could help any reader to follow suit.

TONY STAFFORD

CONTENTS

CHAPTER ONE
Why Handicaps?

The only way to win at racing is to follow the advice given by every successful professional backer from R W Sievier to Alex Bird and to dedicate yourself to the study of form. **If taken in conjunction with other key factors, form works out better in handicaps than in any other type of race.**

Many 'experts' who claim that form is better in non-handicaps (stakes) seem to have an especial weakness for 2 year old races. In my view, next to selling handicaps, these are the most unpredictable of all the races in the calendar.

When I first got interested in racing, I read what I still think is one of the best books ever written on the subject of races for 2 year olds: *Betting To Win* by Supernap, published in 1963. I accepted his argument that: 'Two-year-olds run more truly to form than their elders. They have not had time to become jaded, nor have hard races left an impression on them and made them unwilling to give of their best.' (p14).

I followed two year old racing for almost a decade before I became convinced that two year old form is not very reliable. It is true that two year olds do run to their best—**but it is difficult to know what this is.**

Horses running against other newcomers can often give quite a false impression of their ability. The apparent promise of horses running into a place in a maiden race is frequently belied by subsequent events—because there is no standard for judging such a race, except (possibly) time. Even when the field contains previous winners, at this age horses rarely run often enough to give the backer a clear idea of what kind of course, distance or going they prefer. Many stakes races (including those for older horses) are run at a shambling pace in the early stages, followed by a two furlong dash for the line which is bound to produce misleading results.

Two year olds are no more (and no less) genuine than any other age group. In fact, 'rogues' are individuals and do not belong to any class or age of horse, and their number at all ages is quite small. The most reliable set of horses in racing is not characterised by age group, but by sex (or lack of it)—the geldings (castrated horses) of all ages are the most honest and reliable of types.

As compared to stakes races for any age, handicaps, especially those run over distances up to 8f, are usually run at a good pace. This is because the weaker horses carrying light weights, and receiving up to 2 stone 7 lbs from the top weights, set off at a pace they cannot sustain for the distance. Generally, handicaps attract larger fields, which ensure that there will be a pacemaker.

If you don't believe me just watch a few races of both types. In two-year-old races, the newcomers run 'green' ie they move all over the place out of the stalls, the whole field seeming to sway left and right until they settle down. At that stage, one horse usually sets up a good lead and the rest finish well behind strung out over a considerable distance. Even races involving more experienced competitors are weakly contested more often than not.

Another line of proof is to examine the record of winners of non-handicaps when placed in handicaps. It often happens that early in the season an unexposed three-year-old will win a non-handicap very easily indeed. The 'dark horse' is optimistically entered for a handicap, and surprisingly often is made favourite. Far more often than not, the newcomer runs down the field without ever being in contention—and that is virtually that as far as the horse's subsequent career is concerned.

This happens because non-handicaps (especially those early in the season) are often quite uncompetitive, with a field of unknown quantities. Charitable race reports describe the early pace as 'modest', enabling the winner to conserve his energy for the final two furlong sprint. Entered in a handicap, these horses don't know what's hit them—the lightweights go off at a true pace, and the novice to handicaps is run off his feet in the first 2 furlongs. Even low-grade handicaps are generally quite competitive and run at a true pace, so that the real limitations of a horse are revealed to devastating effect.

Your first golden rule must be: **never follow non-handicap form into a handicap.**

Some successful backers avoid 2 year old races for the reasons given above, but concentrate on the Classic and Group races contested by 3 year olds and upwards. It is true that these races are more closely contested than 2 year old races; we do know something about the horses' preference for course, distance and going; these are top class horses, and the higher the class the more consistent the form; and the betting market on these races is usually quite strong, good odds being available about several horses.

However, there are still a number of drawbacks. Especially in the longer distance races, the pace can be muddling in the early stages, particularly when there is no pacemaker. In the very high class races, you have to attempt to relate English form to that shown in France or Ireland, which is often pure guesswork. Finally, in many of these races, a high-class horse overshadows his rivals and is on offer only at very short prices.

With some sections of the racing public, there is a great deal of snobbery about handicappers. Some racegoers feel that by betting in the Classic races they are somehow associating themselves with the aristocracy of the racing world. If you'd rather have a 3-1 loser in a Classic race than a 4-1 winner in a handicap for this reason, don't read on!

For different reasons, the preoccupation with the Classic and near-Classic races is encouraged by the press. Certain racing writers will dismiss a horse as 'just a handicapper' and indeed large sections of the racing press are filled with speculation about Classic horses and their breeding.

This is because the big money in racing today is derived from breeding. Not that by any scientific standard the stud farms have been very successful: the time recorded by the average Derby winner has barely improved at all over the last 50 years. But they have been a great commercial success, as racehorses come second only to Old Master paintings as a medium for speculation.

Classic horses do look beautiful and often run some extremely impressive races. The emphasis here must be on 'some': Classic horses nowadays tend to be very underraced. They run perhaps half-a-dozen times in all before being rushed off to the paddocks, perhaps half-way through their second season, in case they lose.

You can see that it is correspondingly difficult to form an impression of their real abilities. Give me a sprint handicapper any day—they run their hearts out often under big weights over all types of going and over different courses for season after season.

The Classics are of no interest to me whatsoever—they are just a series of 3 year old non-handicaps, two of which (the Derby and the Oaks) are run over a rather idiosyncratic course (Epsom). In particular the so-called classic trials are just that—a real trial for the punter, with upsets and 'sensations' every year. Who said handicaps were an unreliable betting medium?

To learn to be a handicap expert, you do not need to learn the special skills which take years of experience and a long time working with horses to acquire—to judge conformation, so that you can have a reasonable idea as to whether a raw two year old will 'make up' into a good performer. Some of the best private handicappers I have met do not know one end of a horse from another. But, you may ask, isn't it precisely in handicap racing that we see the greatest number of 'results' for the bookmaker—the unconsidered winners at 50-1, with the 'form' horses coming nowhere?

Many punters think that big gambles are frequent in handicap races and horses are 'laid out' with this in mind. This is no longer true.

Here recent developments in British racing have helped the handicap specialist, although they have made racing less interesting. Racing is much more centralised today than it was 20 years ago: the big trainers' mega-stables with 200 horses dominate the main meetings. It is now comparatively rare for the smaller trainers to win handicaps at the big meetings. The practice of 'laying out' a horse for a handicap at a big meeting seems much less common than it used to be.

This may be for two reasons: starting stalls, the camera patrol and the video make it harder to 'drop out' a horse in the earlier stages of the race and so eventually gain a favourable handicap rating; and the bigger stables as a rule simply can't be bothered to take the trouble. The big trainers simply don't need betting *coups*—in any case with a stable of up to 200 horses they do not always have the time to organise them.

The raising of the minimum weight to be carried in a handicap to 7st 7lbs (from 1962 onwards) has also cut off one possible source of *coups*—the well-prepared horse carrying around 7st was in with a very strong chance, especially in very soft going. As the number of good light-weight jockeys falls, it is quite probable that in the near future the minimum weight may have to be raised still further.

Trainers who are just starting their careers may aim for *coups* in the traditional medium of the selling race. But, even here, since the 1970s and the departure for shores unknown of a master of this kind of operation, the trainer Ken Payne, the bookmakers' intelligence network is now much better developed and the markets are often so weak that it is difficult to place a good bet. Only at major meetings can one be certain of a really strong betting market.

Finally, the bookmaker's intelligence service is often said to be better organised than MI5, though I realise that this is a somewhat dubious compliment. The days of great *coups* planned in secrecy or with trial gallops with different weights to confuse the work watchers are over—and have been for thirty years. There is a simple economic reason for this. The big money in racing is now in breeding not in betting coups—they are simply not worth it for all the time and trouble involved.

All the same, I do agree that often handicaps often do provide 'surprises', **but the answer is to be selective**. There are two kinds of handicaps, at both ends of the racing scale, which are 'traps'.

First, the average handicap at the lesser meetings, *is* usually a lottery. Week after week, you will see the same fairly mediocre animals competing for low-value prizes. Many of them are there to make up the numbers and never win a race. They may run into a place, thus giving rise to unfounded expectations on the part of their ever-optimistic owners. There is an element of 'Buggin's turn' here—one day as a result of sheer persistence or luck in running, even the poorer animals with little visible form will win a race. Usually it will be a long time before they win again and their winning chances at any one time cannot be predicted with any degree of certainty.

Therefore you should concentrate on the better-class handicaps at the leading courses. Not only do better-class horses run much more consistently, but an additional problem with smaller meetings is the weakness of the betting market. Even if you found a good bet in the lowest grade of handicap at the smaller meetings, it would be difficult to do anything about it.

Even a £400 bet is big enough to cause the price to tumble. This is mainly because the modern bookmaker operates more like an accountant than the older generation of bookmakers, such as William Hill, who operated as a gambler in reverse.

Secondly, some of the best publicised handicaps are also a trap for the punter, for various reasons. They are: the Lincoln (no recent form); the Stewards Cup, Goodwood (usually a wide open race); the Extel, Goodwood (usually won by a rapidly-improving horse running unpredictably well in advance of its previous form); the Ebor, York (not enough handicaps for good horses over the 14f distance); the Cambridgeshire (run over an unusual distance, 9f, for which there is little directly relevant form); and the Cesarewitch (few competitive handicaps over 2¼ miles). Avoid these races, and there are plenty of good handicaps at the major meetings which offer sound betting opportunities.

Nor do you need to know anything about breeding. You do not need to get involved in the kind of endless speculation about whether your horse will get the distance which informs so much of the writing about the Classics.

In handicap racing, there is almost always enough information from actual past performances for you to make a reasonable judgement about the most suitable distance for a given horse. Most handicappers have found their distance by their third season. All you need is to follow a simple rule: **to back a horse to do what it has done before**.

The systematic approach I give here applies to handicaps over all distances. I have a preference for sprint handicappers, mainly because they race so often. This may seem odd: in these races, runners are often slowly away; they can get boxed in during the race; and a bad draw may make all the difference. These are problems I admit, but they can be resolved.

The first is important only at some courses. At others the conformation of the course (such as the Hunt Cup course at Ascot, or the 6f course at Goodwood) allows even rather elderly slow starters enough time to recover to be there when it matters.

As to the second factor—on wide, galloping courses or courses with an uphill finish, there is plenty of opportunity to find a good position and less chance of being irretrievably hampered.

Finally, the draw is known in advance and we can decide (the statistics are readily available) to wait for another day if our selection is badly drawn.

In my view these disadvantages are fully outweighed by the fact that nine sprints out of ten are run at a very true pace—far more so than any other category of race. In fact, to go to the other extreme, I am very loath to bet in races over distances greater than 12f—because it is much more difficult to know in advance how the race is going to be run. There is too high a probability that the early pace would not tax an indolent tortoise—the resulting dash for home in the last 2 furlongs can produce most misleading results.

For different reasons, my approach unfortunately does not work for National Hunt racing. I say 'unfortunately' because the atmosphere at most 'over-the-sticks' meetings is more relaxed and enjoyable than at even the lowlier Flat courses.

The reason for its not working is not the obvious one—ie that your selection might fall or be brought down. In the better-class hurdle or steeplechase, this rarely happens to good jumpers. What frequently happens is that the race is really over with about 100 yards to go—the beaten horses are eased, and there is at least 5 lengths between the placed horses. For a system like mine in which 1lb either way (commonly agreed to be equivalent to 1 length over hurdle/steeplechase distances) is the difference between winning or losing, this does make life difficult.

If handicap form is the most reliable, what do you need to know in order to understand how form works?

The key to understanding race form is simple: **learn to read races carefully and draw your own conclusions**. This is an art which takes a great deal of practice, and I doubt if one in ten racegoers ever try to master it (see ch 4). Many other systems, especially those based around backing favourites, depend on what *other* people think—and the systems backer doesn't ever need to watch any races.

You will get far more enjoyment out of racing if you learn to read races properly, and nowadays with S.I.S. and so many televised races which you can video and watch several times, it doesn't take long to acquire the basic skills.

However, you can be a good race reader and still not be any good at picking winners. You not only need to know how well a particular horse ran on this occasion, but also you need to know under what circumstances the horse is capable of reproducing this form. Here a detailed knowledge of the differences between the various racecourses in Britain (see ch 6) and of the racing season (see ch 10) is essential. It is the aim of this book to provide you with this knowledge, so that on the basis of *your* evaluation of previous races you can back your own judgement instead of blindly following that of someone else.

The pattern of the racing season has changed little over the last twenty years apart from All-weather racing. There has been something of a shift away from the early season meetings to the high and late season, but this has had more effect on the Classic horses than on handicappers. Season after season certain handicap races provide a good pointer to success in races later in the season. Some handicaps are regularly won by horses with good form credentials—while others rarely are. If you can identify the former, you are obviously in with a good chance.

But, to begin at the beginning. How is a handicap compiled? How can you compile your own handicap which you think is better than that of the official handicapper?

CHAPTER TWO
How Handicaps are Compiled

'A public handicapper should be a man of independent circumstances, in every sense of the word, and beyond suspicion of accepting illicit compensation for favours received. Attached to no stable, a good judge of the condition of the horse, but with a more intimate knowledge of the dispositions of owners and trainers, he should be a spectator of every race of any importance in the United Kingdom...' (Admiral Rous, *On the Laws and Practice of Horse Racing* 1850 p124).

The essence of handicapping is quite simple. In a handicap race, horses are allocated different weights so that each competitor has a theoretically equal chance of winning. The number of close finishes we see in handicap racing, especially in the high season when there is plenty of form for the handicapper to work on, is a tribute to the skill of the official handicapper.

The generally accepted relation between weight and distance is as follows:
For 5f races: up to a half length = 1 pound; 3/4 length = 2 pounds; 1 length = 3 pounds.
For 6f–8f races: up to half a length = 1 pound; 3/4 length = 2 pounds; 1 length = 2 pounds.
For races of 9 furlongs and over: up to half a length no allowance; 3/4 length = 1 pound; 1 length = 1 pound.

In the present system, all horses are allocated a handicap mark by the official Jockey Club handicappers on a scale 0–140 with each point on this scale representing one pound weight. The top handicapper is on 115, with horses above that being in the Group category; the horses at the bottom of the lowest grade handicaps are around the 40 mark.

Handicap Mark and Handicap Weight

What relation does the handicap mark bear to the amount of weight a horse is required to carry in a given race? At first sight, this is one of the most confusing features of handicap racing and many punters seem to be unaware of the distinction between handicap mark and handicap weight—especially when they see that on the same day a horse may be set to carry top weight in one handicap, and be near the bottom of another. This is because the horse is running in different classes of handicaps. With the exception of nurseries (handicaps for 2 year olds), all handicaps are now graded, from the lowest (for horses rated 0–75) to the highest (0–115).

To give an example. Say we have a horse called MARKS FOLLY, rated at 75, entered in two handicaps, a 0–75 and 0–110. This means that the top horse in each handicap will be rated 75 and 110 respectively. Here are the weights it will carry:

	Handicap Mark	Handicap Weight
THE BRIGHTON HANDICAP (0–75)		
MARKS FOLLY	75	10–0
THE SALISBURY HANDICAP (0–110)		
MARKS FOLLY	75	7–7

Thus the handicap weight carried is no real guide to the handicap mark. This is a simple point, but it is amazing how many punters who bet frequently in handicaps seem to be unaware of the distinction. I have so often seen punters giving a handicap a cursory glance and saying 'X is not carrying much weight and is well in in the handicap'.

Often they are looking at the horses towards the bottom of the handicap, say in the 7–7 to 8–0 mark. But if the handicapper has got the measure of the horse, it does not matter what it is carrying in absolute terms, what matters is its position in the handicap *relative* to other horses.

The handicap mark is further obscured by the fact that under the description of the conditions of the handicap you will sometimes see a line of type: 'Weights raised 3lbs.' An imaginary example will make clear what this means.

When the entries for this race were originally made (usually 5 days before the race for ordinary handicaps, but much longer for some of the big handicaps), the range of weights was as follows (the middle weights are omitted as they are not relevant in this case):

	WEIGHT	MARK
ARTHUR	10–0	90
BELINDA	9–9	85
CAMILLA'S BOY	9–9	85
DAVID	9–7	83
EDGAR PAINTER	9–6	82
FRITILLARY	7–6	54
ZAPATA	7–4	52

Originally, therefore, FRITILLARY on 7–6 and ZAPATA on 7–4, are not eligible, because the lowest weight allowed in a handicap is usually 7–7. The handicap below the eligible point is known as the 'long handicap'—to accommodate horses which at this stage are not eligible but which do have a mark.

At the next stage, the top three horses were withdrawn, so in order to make sure that enough runners are left in the race, the weights were raised 3 lbs, bringing in FRITILLARY and ZAPATA as the bottom weights. The *marks* remain the same but the *weights* are changed, so that the race now looks like this:

	WEIGHT	MARK
DAVID	9–10	83
EDGAR PAINTER	9–9	83
FRITILLARY	7–9	54
ZAPATA	7–7	53

You can see, therefore, that the weight carried is no guide to the handicap mark. Both the daily racing papers, the *Racing Post* and the *Sporting Life*, give the handicap mark.

A Typical Handicap

Now let's look at the conditions of a typical handicap, run at Redcar on 29 May 1989. In the morning newspaper it appears as follows (with some inessential details omitted):

3.15 Zetland Gold Cup Handicap 1¼ miles

> For three year olds and upwards, rated 0–115. Lowest weight 7st 7lbs. Penalties after May 20th, a winner of a race value £5000 6lbs. Closing on May 24th.
>
> Weights raised 9 lbs.

Always read the small print! The main points to extract here are: the grade of the race (0–115); and the conditions for penalties.

First, the line 'Weights raised 9lbs', should alert you to the fact that this may not be as strong a field as you would expect for the highest grade of handicap, a 0–115. And so it was—in fact, the top mark was 92, so this field could have contested a 0–110 or even a 0–100.

Next, the conditions for penalties. They would be incurred after May 20th—this means that the handicap marks were compiled on the basis of form shown up to that date. Thus a horse could have won by, say, 10 lengths pulling up, yet would still only incur a penalty of 6 lbs.

This is one of the gaps in the handicapper's armoury that can be exploited by the astute backer. A horse may have won so well that the penalty in no way reflects the merits of the win that entailed it. The trainer will run the horse carrying a penalty, expecting that the handicapper will raise the horse to a much higher mark when he assesses the value of that win.

Alternatively, the horse may have run well without winning in a race run after May 20th. This is a less clear-cut case, but it does mean that the private handicapper has an advantage over his official counterpart.

One other 'loophole' in the handicap system which unfortunately is of no advantage to the backer, is that at present horses are required to run only one race before they can be entered for handicaps. Until the mid-sixties, the rule was that they had to be run in three races, thus giving the handicapper a reasonable idea of their abilities. A case of a horse being able to enter (and win) a handicap in this way was TYRIAN BELLE (1988). In this situation, both the private and the official handicapper are equally in the dark.

Weight for Age

In the example of a typical handicap just analysed, all the runners are of the same age, three year olds. How does the handicapper make allowances for horses of different ages competing against each other?

The scale of Weight for Age drawn up by Admiral Rous in 1850 (and slightly amended since) sets out the amount of weight a horse will receive from older horses. I am only concerned with 3 year olds racing against their elders, as 2 year olds rarely if ever compete against 3 year olds in handicaps. Here is the table of allowances for 3 year olds.

WEIGHT FOR AGE: AMOUNT TO BE RECEIVED BY 3 YEAR OLDS FROM OLDER HORSES*

5f	13	12	11	10	9	8	7	6	5	4	3	2	1	0	0
6f	15	14	13	12	11	10	9	8	7	6	5	4	3	2	1
7f	16	15	14	13	12	11	10	9	8	7	6	5	4	3	2
8f	18	17	16	15	14	13	12	11	10	9	8	7	6	5	4
9f	18	17	16	15	14	13	12	11	10	9	8	7	6	5	4
10f	19	18	17	16	15	14	13	12	11	10	9	8	7	6	5
11f	20	19	18	17	16	15	14	13	12	11	10	9	8	7	6
12f	21	19	18	17	16	15	14	13	12	11	10	9	8	7	6

* Reading the table across, the first figure (13) is the amount in pounds to be received in March; every subsequent figure applies to every fortnightly period thereafter.

You will see from the scale that at the beginning of the season in a 5f race a 3 year old will receive 13lbs from an older horse, but by the middle of October they are on a par. As the younger horse progresses physically it receives a smaller allowance from its elders.

It is vital to understand that the scale is concerned with physical development and not racing ability. Thus, if a 3 year old and an older horse are considered to be of equal ability, they will be on the same handicap mark, but the 3 year old will receive the allowance specified in the Weight for Age scale, to compensate for his less mature physical development. If he stays on the same handicap mark, when he is a 4 year old he will have to make exactly the same concession to a 3 year old.

Thus two horses on the *same* mark but of *different* ages will carry *different* weights. This is another case of the weight carried being misleading—what you need to know is the mark. For the moment, the weight carried is of no interest to us.

Types of Handicaps

Most handicaps are for 3 year olds only, or 'all-aged' ie for 3 year olds and upwards. There are three other kinds: selling handicaps; apprentice handicaps; and 'nurseries'.

Selling handicaps are possibly the worst type of race from a betting point of view in the entire racing calendar, with the possible exception of plates for two year old maidens. As a rule they are contested, if that is the right word, by the most moderate animals in the racing world. They also offer a real opportunity for a *coup*—some trainers used to specialise in using this kind of race for a fairly substantial gamble.

Once in a while a really good handicapper emerges from a selling handicap—for instance, NOT SO SILLY(1987). This can only be recognised with the wisdom of hindsight, however, and it is essential to wait until such a rapidly-improving horse has made the progression from selling races.

If you must have a bet in a selling handicap, the only advice I can give you—apart from 'Don't'—is to look for a horse which has run in a non-selling race of any description and shown the slightest glimmer of form. To run an undistinguished ninth or tenth in a non-seller may be good enough to win in a seller.

Apprentice handicaps are viewed with great scepticism by most punters, not always for very good reasons. **I must admit that I have rarely found a betting opportunity in this type of race,** but that is more to do with the type of animal which competes—usually older handicappers of mediocre quality. An astute trainer may sometimes enter a penalised winner for an apprentice handicap in which he can be ridden by a good claiming apprentice. **The difference between a 5 lb claimer and a 7 lb claimer is usually much more than 2 lbs, in terms of the assistance they can give to the horse.**

Nursery handicaps or 'nurseries', handicaps confined to 2 year olds are a different matter altogether.

Until 1978 the nursery season did not start until the beginning of August. It was then put forward to the beginning of July, so that in 1987, for example, the first nursery at a big meeting was on 11 July at York (Race 1650. In all the race numbers in this book, I use the official form book number—this is published in *Raceform Handicap Book* and *Raceform Midweek*). From around the Goodwood meeting, there are 6f nurseries, and later in the season 7f and even 8f events.

Backers are often warned that an interest in nurseries will inevitably lead to the bankruptcy courts. This is because it quite often happens that a moderate to average two year old is given a few easy runs in poorly-contested non-handicap races, and is then placed to advantage with a low weight in a nursery. Usually this is the limit of his ability, and the trainer has done well to get one win out of the horse for that year.

I agree that this is a danger, but it usually happens in the lower class nurseries—in the better contested events, especially at Newmarket, the form is as reliable as it is in any sprint handicap. Most years if the weather holds at the end of the season, you can find one or two excellent opportunities, if you treat a nursery as just another sprint handicap.

More particularly, I would recommend the following simple rules for betting in nurseries:

1. As in other handicaps, never follow non-handicap form into a handicap. I say this although I get the impression that winners of 2 year old stakes do have a better record in handicaps than do their elders—but on the other hand, it still isn't very good;

2. Confine your bets to sprint distances—5f and 6f. In my view, it is asking too much of a 2 year old to race over 7f and 8f, and in any case there is little form to go on;

3. Only consider nursery form shown from the Doncaster St.Leger meeting onwards—in practice, I have found that nursery form from meetings earlier than this is unreliable.

There aren't enough nurseries for you to consider betting solely in this type of event, but if you do get really interested, I would recommend you read Will O'Hanlon, *Juveniles Handicapped!—An Investigation of the Nursery Season.*

CHAPTER THREE
Compiling a Private Handicap: Examples

Having considered the general principles of compiling a private handicap, now let us look at a series of examples to illustrate the problems involved.

All are taken from the 1988 season. I begin on the second day of the first meeting, at Doncaster, with the Leger Way Handicap. As a (0–75) it is of a low grade which I would not consider later in the season, but it illustrates certain points about making a handicap and it has none of the minor but irritating complications which will become evident in later examples.

Here is the bare result:

Race 49* 25 March 1988 DONCASTER 8f (round) (0–75) soft

PRINCE MERANDI	5–9–0	61**	—
QUALITAIR FLYER	6–8–2	49	neck
MILAN FAIR	4–9–6	67	4 lengths
LYRICAL LOVER	4–8–13	60	3 lengths
MIAMI BAY	4–8–9	56	3 lengths
SYLVAN ORIENT	4–8–2	49	3 lengths

* This is the race number from the official form book (it appears in *Raceform Handicap Book*).
** this column gives the official handicap mark.

How should we adjust the handicap marks to reflect the result of this race? For convenience here again is the weight and distance table:

For 5f races: up to a half length = 1 pound; ¾ length = 2 pounds; 1 length = 3 pounds.

For 6f–8f races: up to half a length = 1 pound; ¾ length = 2 pounds; 1 length = 2 pounds;

For races of 9 furlongs and over up to half a length no allowance; ¾ length = 1 pound; 1 length = 1 pound.

I work out quarter and half lengths by simple multiplication, rounding the result down to a whole number ie a 5f race on good going, 2¾ lengths = 8 pounds.

If handicapping were merely an arithmetic exercise it would be a simple matter to re-calculate the handicap marks according to the allowances given above. If it were, handicapping could be done entirely by computers!

It isn't, **because the 'arithmetical' result leaves two questions unanswered: does the winning distance reflect the real margin of superiority? does the result show that PRINCE MERANDI has improved or that the losers have deteriorated?**

We can give an answer to the first question using our reading of the race; as to the second, we are not yet in a position to give an answer.

The race was decided at around the 'distance' (240 yards from the winning post). PRINCE MERANDI took the lead, and ran on to hold the challenge of QUALITAIR FLYER who was ridden out but always held. From this point the others posed no problem and simply ran out their race. Of the 'also rans' only LYRICAL LOVER showed much progress—but was perhaps flattering to deceive. In answer to the first question, I felt that the winner always had about 1 length in hand; and that the position of the third and those behind should not be considered literally.

This is quite common in early season handicaps—two horses run competitively against each other, and the rest aren't really in it.

To answer the second question, I consider that the second horse has run to his mark, and I uprate the first by the amount I consider he has in hand—here 1 length, ie 1 pound. The third and fourth I tentatively downgrade by 4 pounds; the fifth and sixth by 7 pounds.

The result to include our amended marks is as follows:

Race 49 25 March 1988 DONCASTER 8f (round) (0–75) soft

PRINCE MERANDI	5-9-0	61	–	63
QUALITAIR FLYER	6-8-2	49	neck	49
MILAN FAIR	4-9-6	67	4 lengths	(63)
LYRICAL LOVER	4-8-13	60	3 lengths	(56+)
MIAMI BAY	4-8-9	56	3 lengths	(49)
SYLVAN ORIENT	4-8-2	49	3 lengths	(42)

The + sign after LYRICAL LOVER's rating means that I consider it possible that he is better than the bare rating suggests. The brackets indicate that these ratings are provisional.

So far, we have arrived at a new set of ratings. How reliable are they?

At least 7 of the 24 runners were noted as 'backward', that is, unfit. Perhaps, therefore, the leading horses just happened to be the fittest on the day. Only time will tell—in the meantime, I consider the form from this race unreliable. In fact, you will find very few races reliable at this stage of the season—and even later on, there will be a few which are unreliable, but for different reasons.

What did the official handicapper make of the result? The new handicap ratings are published in the official Jockey Club *Racing Calendar* but you can find out just as quickly and far more easily by looking at the *Raceform Handicap Book* on Thursdays, or the daily racing papers on Fridays. As the original race was on a Friday, the amended ratings did not appear until 13 days later.

Race 49 25 March 1988 DONCASTER 8f (round) (0–75) soft

PRINCE MERANDI	5-9-0	61	–	63	66*
QUALITAIR FLYER	6-8-2	49	neck	49	53
MILAN FAIR	4-9-6	67	4 lengths	(63)	
LYRICAL LOVER	4-8-13	60	3 lengths	(56+)	
MIAMI BAY	4-8-9	56	3 lengths	(49)	
SYLVAN ORIENT	4-8-2	49	3 lengths	(42)	

*The official handicapper's re-ratings

At this stage the official handicapper's ratings (in the far right hand column) only apply to the first two, as the other ratings have been left unchanged. Now let us abstract from this my ratings and those of the official handicapper for purposes of comparison:

HANDICAP RATINGS AT 7 APRIL 1988

HORSE	1	2	3	4
PRINCE MERANDI	61	63	66	−3
QUALITAIR FLYER	49	49	53	−4

MILAN FAIR	67	(63)	67	(−4)
LYRICAL LOVER	60	(56+)	60	(−4+)
MIAMI BAY	56	(49)	56	(−7)
SYLVAN ORIENT	49	(42)	49	(−7)

COLUMN 1 = Previous rating
COLUMN 2 = New rating: my handicap
COLUMN 3 = New rating: official handicap
COLUMN 4 = Discrepancy between my handicap and official handicap (ie Column 2—Column 3)

You will see that according to my rating (column 2) I consider that PRINCE MERANDI should carry 3 lbs less than the official re-rating (column 3). I express this as '−3' (ie column 2 minus column 3), the negative sign clearly expressing my negative evaluation of his current position on the official handicap. If I had considered that his victory deserved re-rating to 69, and the official mark was still 66, then he would appear as '+3' in column 4, ie well in with regard to the official handicap.

In the case examined above, *Raceform Private Handicap* does the sum the other way round, and rates PRINCE MERANDI as '+3'. It is purely a matter of convention, but the negative sign is a clearer indicator of a negative estimate of the horse's position in the handicap: it really doesn't matter, providing you follow one system consistently.

What is the reason for the discrepancy? It is that the official handicapper read the race differently: he took the third horse, MILAN FAIR, as the 'marker', and raised the second, QUALITAIR FLYER, 4 lbs for the 4 lengths between them, and the winner 5 lbs for the 4 lengths and a neck. I thought that the handicapper was being rather cautious—but in his position, at this stage of the season, he has to err on the side of caution. I frequently find that the largest discrepancies (in a negative direction) between my ratings and those of the handicapper are at this stage of the season.

The handicapper has also only altered the ratings of the top two. For obvious reasons, he cannot quickly downgrade unplaced horses, as after a few runs they would be on a zero or even negative mark! As I do not have to guard against possible *coups* planned in this way, I tend to downgrade the ratings more quickly, but the bracket placed round the figures is a warning sign that this is a provisional rating.

However, all this is rather theoretical—we are both in the dark until some of these horses run again. As it happens, there was a quick feedback on the result of this race. PRINCE MERANDI appeared at Kempton (Race 108) in a 9f (0–100). This was not too dissimilar a contest in terms of distance, course configuration, or going (soft in both cases).

Because he ran again before the handicapper adjusted the marks, he was obliged to carry a 5 lbs penalty for his Doncaster win. This meant that he effectively had to run to a 66 mark to win—in our appreciation his mark was 63 ie he had to find a further 3 pounds to win. As it later turned out, the handicapper was to raise him to 66: so this was a good test.

He was top-rated by the form expert of the *Sporting Life* and perhaps for that reason opened as favourite—in our view, quite unjustified. One of the great values of a private handicap is that it will quickly identify the favoured horses which are in fact badly in at the weights, as seemed to be the case here. Here is the result:

Race 118 4 April 1988 KEMPTON 9f
(0–100) soft
Weights raised 3 lbs

KINGSFOLD FLAME	5–9–5	79	—
COUNT TREVISIO	4–8–11	51	2½
PRINCE MERANDI	5–8–6	61	½
LILY MAB	4–8–1	56	hd
GURTEEN BOY	6–8–6	66	1½
CI SIAMO	4–8–13	73	3

PRINCE MERANDI ran well enough in this race to be third, but in my view was anchored by the penalty, going down three lengths. This seemed to confirm my judgement, and I left his mark at 63. A penalised horse which runs like this is very helpful in my search for a 'marker' ie a horse which runs to its rating—later in the season, there will be other pointers, but at this early stage I was grateful for this sign.

Given that PRINCE MERANDI has run to his mark of 63, how are the other marks to be allocated? The winner led from 2 furlongs out and ran on strongly, to win by something more than the bare margin; the second plodded on honestly, but with no hope of success. Working upwards, therefore, I raised COUNT TREVISIO'S mark by 1 pound for the half-a-length he beat PRINCE MERANDI; and allowed the winner '4 pounds plus' for the 3 lengths he was in front. Working downwards, I considered that LILY MAB was on a par with PRINCE MERANDI; and downgraded the others accordingly.

One way that form experts try to get round the problem of there being so little form in the early weeks of the season is by using what is called 'collateral form'.

Say if PRINCE MERANDI had won his second race, running to a mark of 66 or even higher, and beat BILLYS BOY by 4 lengths at the same weights. If QUALITAIR FLYER appeared after this second race, and met BILLYS BOY at comparable weights, it would seem logical to argue that although QUALITAIR FLYER and BILLYS BOY had not previously raced against each other, using PRINCE MERANDI as a standard of comparison ('on a line through' is the racing jargon) he would be at least 4 pounds in hand.

I find that although it appears logical collateral form tends to be rather unreliable—it is based on a rather literal reading of weights and distances, **whereas handicapping is very much a matter of judgement.**

One other expedient is used in these early weeks. A time value is computed for each horse—this has the merit of being more objective, if a horse records a good time there is no argument about it. *But*, and it is a big 'but', time values recorded on going which is soft or worse are in my opinion very speculative indeed—and this is the kind of going you are likely to get early in the season.

You will have noticed that at the top of the results table I have included 'Weights raised 3 pounds'. Does this enter into our analysis of the result? As I have explained earlier, the handicap marks are obviously unaffected. However, in some races you will see that the weights will have been raised as much as 20 lbs. If that were the case in this race, the top weight of 10–0 would be on a mark of 71. Therefore the race is of poorer class than you would normally expect for a 0–100. **So if the weights are raised by a stone or more, I tend to rate the class of handicap lower.**

It is also worth noting the top mark in a handicap. If the top mark in a 0–100 handicap is say 7lbs or more less than 100, ie 93 downwards, then this is a weak 0–100 race.

Here is the result:

Race 118 4 April 1988 KEMPTON 9f (0–100) soft
Weights raised 3 lbs

KINGSFOLD FLAME	5–9–5	79	—	83 +
COUNT TREVISIO	4–8–11	71	2½	72
PRINCE MERANDI	5–8–6	61	½	63
LILY MAB	4–8–1	56	hd	56
GURTEEN BOY	6–8–6	66	1½	(62)
CI SIAMO	4–8–13	73	3	(66)

There is one further point which can be illustrated using these ratings. When the official handicapper assessed this race he agreed with me (for the first time!) by putting COUNT TREVISIO up to 72, so in my book he was now '−' ie, levels.

But on 12 April he appeared in a Newmarket handicap running off the 71 mark—this was because the weights were compiled before the mark could be revised. He was, therefore, '+1' in our ratings, the first horse to achieve this distinction! I was not confident enough about the value of any of the ratings calculated so far to consider selecting him.

After that detailed examination of the consequences of one race, let's return to Doncaster, to look at the Will Scott Handicap (Race 51: 5f 0–90). The result was as follows:

Race 51 25 March 1988 DONCASTER 5f (0–90) soft

NO BEATING HARTS	5–8–2 (2 ow)	59	—	64
PROFIT A PRENDRE	4–8–4	63	¾	63
JONDEBE BOY	4–9–6	79	1½	(75)
JOVEWORTH	5–8–4 (‡7)	70	1	(66)
SPITZABIT	4–8–7	66	1	(62)
FOURWALK	4–10–0	87	¾	(84)

Before looking at the race, let me put out of the way two complications.

Firstly, '2 ow' in brackets after the winner's weight refers to the amount of overweight carried. NO BEATING HARTS was set to carry 8–0, but his jockey couldn't make that weight, and put up 2 lbs overweight. Always remember that the weights published in the results are the weights actually *carried,* not the weights set.

Secondly, the alert reader will have noticed that PROFIT A PRENDRE and JOVEWORTH carried the same weights, but have different handicap marks. Don't panic—the British handicapping system has not collapsed in chaos! JOVEWORTH was ridden by apprentice J A Glover, who claimed an apprentice allowance of 7lbs, bringing the weight carried down by that amount.

What of the race itself? This was a good example of the importance of judgement. The official form book and the press commented that PROFIT A PRENDRE had run on well in the final furlong. It didn't look like that to me at all: I thought that he was 'flattering to deceive' as he ran on through beaten horses without either being under pressure himself or putting pressure on the winner. I was strengthened in my opinion, by reading the official form book's report that 6 out of the 15 runners had been 'backward'.

So how to deal with the result? I decided to read it quite literally, allowing the winner 3 lbs for the ¾ length winning margin and 2 lbs for the overweight ie 5 lbs overall. As a general rule, I tend to ignore overweight carried by placed horses, unless they run well. But if a horse *wins* well, you should allow for the overweight in making your calculations. So if a horse carries 2 lbs overweight, and you estimate his winning margin as being the equivalent of 4lbs, then you should re-rate him by 6lbs.

When the amount of overweight carried is quite small, I tend to take it at face value and allow for it pound for pound. In some races, however, ludicrous amounts of overweight are carried, up to 8 lbs or so, and it is impossible to know how to assess this—fortunately it doesn't happen at the big meetings which I am interested in.

Also I discounted the apprentice allowance, assuming that the horse ran 7lbs worse than if he had had a regular jockey. As JOVEWORTH was out of the frame anyway, this was not a serious problem. This is not a hard and fast rule, by the way (see ch 7).

In assessing this result, the official handicapper also looked optimistically at PROFIT A PRENDRE's performance.

HANDICAP RATINGS AT 14 APRIL 1988

NO BEATING HARTS	59	64	68	−4
PROFIT A PRENDRE	63	63	67	−4

So far, both the races I have looked at represent one fairly common type of early season race—there are really only two horses in at the finish. Another very common type appeared at the same day at Kempton, in the Rosebery Handicap:

Race 120 4 April 1988 KEMPTON 10f (0–115) soft
Weights raised 3 lbs

FOUZ	5–8–1 (1 ow)	78	—
SHEER NECTAR	5–7–7	69	5
MR PINTIPS	4–9–4	96	3
GENOBRA	4–9–4	96	2
CRY FOR THE CLOWN	4–9–10	102	nk
JAZETAS	5–8–5	83	hd

To begin with, a minor complication. FOUZ actually carried 8–1, as his jockey weighed in 1 lb overweight, so this will have to be taken into account in any calculations we make.

FOUZ had to be pulled right out to find an opening, but when he did 2 furlongs out, he came away to win easily. From that point, this was a one horse race—SHEER NECTAR toiled on, but was comfortably held, and the others were not in contention. Before the race this looked a competitive high class handicap, and most of the field looked fairly fit—so this is quite an impressive victory. But how do I rate it?

Here there is no obvious 'marker'—all I can do is to make the big assumption that SHEER NECTAR ran to her mark, and allow FOUZ 6lbs for the 5 lengths, add 1 lb for the overweight, and, to show that he is probably better than the mere rating, a ' + ' sign to indicate that he may well be capable of a better performance than this.

Race 120 4 April 1988 KEMPTON 10f (0–115) soft
Weights raised 3 lbs

FOUZ	5–8–1 (1 ow)	78	—	85+
SHEER NECTAR	5–7–7	69	5	69
MR PINTIPS	4–9–4	96	3	(92)
GENOBRA	4–9–4	96	2	(92)
CRY FOR THE CLOWN	4–9–10	102	nk	(95)
JAZETAS	5–8–5	83	hd	(76)

After the handicapper had finished puzzling over what for him must have been a nightmare, he came up with the following:

HANDICAP RATINGS AT 14 APRIL 1988

FOUZ	78	85+	88	− 3+
SHEER NECTAR	69	69	74	− 5
CRY FOR THE CLOWN	102	(95)	101	(− 6)
JAZETAS	83	(76)	83	(− 7)

There are two points to note here. The handicapper had taken the third horse, MR PINTIPS, as the marker, and raised SHEER NECTAR 5 lbs for 5 lengths, and FOUZ 10lbs for 8 lengths, allowing 2 lbs for that incalculable amount in hand. If I thought the form of this race was reliable (which I don't because of the going and time of the season), then FOUZ should be able to defy a 7lbs penalty.

Secondly, the handicapper had relented for the first time this season in a race I had assessed. CRY FOR THE CLOWN went down 1 lb in the ratings, presumably because if he didn't he would always be carrying such welterweights, without being able to win.

Now I come to three early season handicaps run on good going, which eliminates the major obstacle to reliability on the part of the earlier ones.

Race 186 8 April 1988 KEMPTON 6f (0–90) 17 runners good
Weights raised 2 lbs

ONE LINER	4–9–3	77	—	82+
GREENHILL JAZZ TIME	4–8–7	67	1	67+
VORTRACK	4–7–9	60	3	(56)
START-RITE	4–9–10	84	¾	(80)
LUNA BID	5–9–6	80	¾	(76)
FOOLISH TOUCH	6–8–10	70	4	(63)

ONE LINER was ridden out to win after coming to the front inside the final furlong—this wasn't a scintillating finish, but I felt that he had something in hand. However, was this a reliable race?

On the minus side, the first six were spread out over 9½ lengths; and there was no 'obvious' marker from previous races. PROFIT A PRENDRE had run on the second day of the Doncaster meeting. Even if you didn't share my view of his running in that race, **why did the punters take the 7–2? Although he had won twice over this distance, he had _never_ won on good going.** Here he rather inconsiderately ran down the field, as although I certainly didn't expect him to win, I thought he might run on in the same fashion and give us a clue to the abilities of the others.

Most of the races so far have had fields of over 15 runners, which usually ensures a reasonable gallop. This was no exception, but the first race on good going was also won in a good time, a _Raceform_ figure of 70. **So there were two**

pointers to this being a reliable race—going and time.
At this point, I will look at the vexed question of race times. Under certain circumstances, I don't think they are of much use. Time experts ingeniously attempt to compensate for heavy going but I don't find their allowances very convincing so that **I don't take any notice of times recorded on heavy going.**

Nor do I pay any attention to times for races of 7f and over, as these races are often not truly run throughout. So this leaves 5f and 6f races, on good going.

Even this is not a simple matter. Only electric timing is 100% reliable, and this is available at only 15 out of the 35 Flat courses . Once you have a reliable time, this has to be related to a standard time for the course and distance, before you can make any comparisons with times from other courses.

Standard times are to be found in *Raceform*, the Official Form Book. Even this is not a simple matter—if you wanted to compile your own standard times, you couldn't do so with any reliability simply by taking an average of say 20 times for the same course, distance and going. It would be necessary to calculate a 'moving average', to take into account longer term trends in the times recorded. For example, the official form book gives a standard time of 72.60 seconds for 6f on the Newmarket July Course for 1975, 72.00 seconds in 1983.

Rather than get involved in these complications, I rely on the calculations given in *Raceform Handicap Book*, which compiles a very reliable index of time figures—I consider that a figure of 65 is a minimum qualifying figure for a race to be considered reliable, when betting in the higher class of handicap racing. Conversely, in this class of race, a time figure below 65 is usually a very reliable indicator that the form should be considered very carefully; and a time figure below 50 means that this was definitely not a competitively run race. If the winner of such a race is made favourite next time out, this is a definite case of a 'false favourite', which does *not* have a good chance on form.

The winner was ridden out to win after coming to the front inside the final furlong—this wasn't an impressive win, but I felt that the winner did have something in hand. All in all, this was on the borderline as a reliable race, but I had only one reservation about the next race.

Newmarket form is second only to Royal Ascot form throughout the season, so here it was the best. The going was good, and from the opening day of the first meeting, the Craven, I record the following:

Race 217 12 April 1988 NEWMARKET 7f (0–110) 3 year olds good
Weights raised 1 lb

BOLD CITADEL	9–1	96	—
TOP DREAM	7–2 (2 ow)	74	nk
GLOWING REPORT	8–11	92	¾
RISING DEXY	7–3 (‡7)	77	d.h.
RAYKOUR	9–5	100	nk
TURBO SPEED	7–11 (1 ow)	77	1½

What a finish! Only 3 lengths covered the first six, as in a blanket finish they were all driven out to the line. BOLD CITADEL seemed squeezed for room, but came with a strong late finish to get up on the line. RAYKOUR was reported as running on well at the finish—in fact, there was an official inquiry into his running. I couldn't see this at all—I thought he ran on but was held.

The race was run at a true pace in its earlier stages, so this was no 2 furlong dash for the post. The recorded time for the race was quite reasonable, so I considered this to be the first race which looked reliable. How are the ratings to be amended?

As the result stands, 6 lbs (the equivalent of 3 lengths at this distance) covers the first 6; and I distribute this as follows.

I give the winner 4 lbs because of his style of winning—if he had taken the lead at the furlong pole and driven out to the finish, I would have made this only 1 or 2 lbs, but I thought he definitely had something in hand. The next 4 I assume all ran to their marks, but I give 2 lbs to TOP DREAM for his overweight; a question mark against RAYKOUR because there was some uncertainty (though not in my mind) about his performance; and TURBO SPEED, the only one of this group slightly outpaced, I downgrade 2 lbs.

The amended result looks as follows:

Race 217 12 April 1988 NEWMARKET 7f (0–110) 3 year olds good
Weights raised 1 lb

BOLD CITADEL	9–1	96	—	100
TOP DREAM	7–2 (2 ow)	74	nk	76
GLOWING REPORT	8–11	92	¾	92
RISING DEXY	7–3 (‡7)	77	d.h.	77
RAYKOUR	9–5	100	nk	100?
TURBO SPEED	7–11 (1 ow)	77	1½	(73)

Comparing my rating with the handicapper's view of the race:

BOLD CITADEL	100	100	—
TOP DREAM	76	77	− 1
RAYKOUR	100	103	− 3?

Quite a close fit, really, although I thought that the official handicapper was taking no chances with RAYKOUR who, after all, had not yet won a handicap.

As the season progresses, I find that my ratings and those of the official handicapper converge. This does not mean that there will be no opportunities—in fact, it is the smaller discrepancies which are, paradoxically, more significant. In fact, if I find that a horse is 6 or more pounds better in with the handicapper, then I consider that I have probably misjudged the race completely!

The only reservation I had about BOLD CITADEL's race was that none of the runners could be taken as a 'marker'—two-year-old form is notoriously unreliable as a guide to the next season.

There was a race at this meeting at which this deficiency was supplied, and, better still, it included two 'markers' and a horse for which I had a rating.

Race 228 14 April NEWMARKET 12f (0–110) good

FIRST DIVISION	5–8–2	82	—
VOUCHSAFE	6–7–12	78	sh hd
ROUSHAYD	4–9–4	98	4
PROFESSIONAL GIRL	4–9–6	100	nk
GREENHILLS JOY	5–8–9 (4x)	89	hd
CHAUVE SOURIS	5–9–10	104	4

FIRST DIVISION had been in my notebook as an accelerating type since 1986. Six days previously he had run on well at Kempton, so he was − + in my book (this looks confusing but what it means is: level with the official handicap mark (−), but probably better than this (+)). In a reasonably run race, he was held up at the back of the field and ran on very strongly to catch VOUCHSAFE on the line, to win (literally) by about a centimetre as the judges deliberated over the print for a good twenty minutes.

The significant pointers here were VOUCHSAFE and GREENHILLS JOY. The former always ran very gamely and was often in the frame, but had only got his head in front twice. This is unfortunate for his connections, but a godsend to the handicapper. GREENHILLS JOY was anchored by the 4 lbs penalty, and as he was beaten 4 lengths, it suggested he had run to his pre-penalty mark of 85. I kept their marks the same; allowed FIRST DIVISION 2 lbs for a win of this style; and amended the others accordingly. Everything seemed to have worked out to the pound here, but only time would tell.

In this race, I had considered an accelerating type from 1986, FIRST DIVISION. Now for the first race of the season in which I spotted an improving 3 year old with a good turn of foot.

Race 467 2 May KEMPTON 10f (0–90) 3 year olds good

STATEN ISLAND	8–1 (‡5,5x)	70	—
VALLEY OF DANUTA	9–7	85	½
DOCTOR RHYTHM	8–6	70	4
KNOCK KNOCK	7–7	57	nk
TRUE QUEEN	8–8	72	s.h.
NATIVE KNIGHT	8–6	72	1

There was a good sized field of 17 runners for this race with the top mark of 85 in a 0–90 meaning that this was a competitive race for the grade.

Willie Carson rode a brilliant race on the winner, waiting in front, and quickening at the finish to win comfortably. The winning margin was only half a length, but I reckoned it could easily have been four. Accordingly, I raised his mark to 74.

In his next race, the 12 furlong Ultramar Handicap (0–110) at Newbury on 13 May, he was set to run off 75. This was because he was carrying a 6lbs penalty for his Kempton victory, a penalty added to an earlier mark of 69. Therefore, he was only 1lb worse in with the official handicap—an attractive mark for a rapidly improving three year old.

In the final example in this chapter, there is a significant difference between my evaluation of a horse's performance and that made by the official handicapper, which offers the private handicapper clear opportunities.

Race 1123 10 June SANDOWN (0–90) 3 year olds good

HELLO VAIGLY	9–6 (5x)	86	—
HIP HIP HURRY	7–13	65	¾
KAWWAS	8–13	79	3
ISLA BRIDGE	9–5	85	¾
BATCHWORTH DANCER	7–10 (‡5)	67	1 ½
SARNIA SOUND	8–3 (1 ow)	68	hd

On the face of it, not a particularly impressive victory, the margin being only three-quarters of a length. In my view of the race, however, HELLO VAIGLY came with a strong run at the distance and was absolutely full of running at the finish—a very good performance by the jockey, W. Swinburn, to win by such a narrow margin.

For once, I disagreèd with *Raceform Note-Book's* then senior race reader, John Sharratt, who wrote about the winner: 'Off the bit inside the final furlong, he needed hard driving close to home'. Here you have to trust your own judgement, and I thought that the winner had a considerable amount in hand without being really pushed to win. In fact, I raised the winner's mark by 8lbs, to 94.

The official handicapper seemed to agree with me, that HELLO VAIGLY had something in hand, by raising his mark to 90. Here you can appreciate the difficulty of his position—the standard allowance for a winning margin of ¾ length at this distance is 1lb, so in raising the winner's mark by 4lbs, he was making a reasonable allowance for the bare result's not reflecting the amount the winner had in hand. **Even if he completely agreed with my reading of the race, how could he possibly increase the winner's mark by 8lbs?** The trainer and owner of the winner would be fully entitled to complain of the harshness of his decision.

Therefore, in my book, HELLO VAIGLY was 4lbs in hand of the official handicap, and could offer a good betting opportunity later in the season. In the next race (1617), the Addison Tools Handicap, an 8f (0–115) race for 3 year olds, run at Newmarket on 7 July, he was a very good bet indeed. His main competitor was FOREIGN SURVIVOR, carrying a 7lbs penalty for winning the Britannia Stakes at the Royal Ascot meeting, which made him − 2 in my book.

HELLO VAIGLY ran exactly the same race, to win by three quarters of a length, but this time my evaluation of this victory and that of the official handicapper coincided exactly, as we both raised him 5lbs to 95. I felt that the handicapper had now caught up with HELLO VAIGLY, and in his next race this proved to be the case.

In conclusion, the aim of making a private handicap is not so that you can bet in every handicap, but so that you can identify those horses which are 'well in' in relation to the official handicap. This does not mean that they are always a' + ' in relation to the handicap—even 2 or 3lbs out of the handicap may mean that if they are the accelerating type, they are in with a good chance compared to the other horses.

During the course of the season, if you concentrate on the major meetings, you will assess around 140 races. In most seasons you will identify about 15 horses which show that burst of acceleration which can keep them one step ahead of the official handicapper. This may not seem many, but in Chapter 10, you will see that it is enough to ensure a good profit over the season.

Once a sprint handicapper has shown this kind of acceleration, he (or more usually 'it') can retain this ability till aged 9 or even 10. Thus, he may win a series of races as a 5 year old in this way until the official handicapper gets his measure. The next two seasons may be relatively unfruitful as he is running off a mark which is in fact too high for him. But after running unplaced off this mark, the handicapper is obliged to gradually reduce his mark. If he is fit and has retained his old ability, the horse can perfectly will win a series of races again (for example, CHAPLINS CLUB in 1985 and 1988).

This is where the value of keeping your records over a long period will pay handsome dividends. You can look back to the mark from which a horse won two or even three years ago—this may be as much as a stone below the mark from which he has just won convincingly: clearly, he has a margin in hand to win again before the handicapper can get his measure this time.

In this approach to handicapping, interpretation of the way the race was run is the key. The next chapter analyses the vital art of race reading.

CHAPTER FOUR

The Art of Race Reading

The difference, therefore, between any private handicap and the official handicap lies in their different *interpretation* of a race. Did the winner win easily, with something 'in hand' for the future, or was he tested to the limits of his ability? Was this a truly run race, which should give a reliable result—or was it run at a false pace in the early stages, so that the result is almost certainly misleading?

To see how much you can learn from an intelligent 'reading' of a race, look through the reports in *Raceform Note-Book*. The race-readers' reports are based on many years' experience, but anyone with reasonable eyesight and, more importantly, *concentration* can learn to be a reasonable race-reader in a fairly short time. It doesn't take the special skills involved in attempting to judge conformation, or Classic looks, which can only be learned by working with horses for quite a long time.

Given that the race is the whole point of the sport, I am surprised how few racegoers really attempt to learn the art of race-reading. On the racecourse itself, many punters crowd into the bars to watch the racing on the TV screens.

Perhaps the modern racing fan is spoilt. Until the 1950s, there were no broadcast commentaries at the racecourses themselves, so the racegoer *had* to read the race for himself rather than rely on the commentary.

Until the last decade only the major races were televised. Although its extensive coverage enables the racing fan to watch many more races than he would be able to unless he is wealthy and leisured enough to attend all the major meetings, TV is in some respects a distinct second best to the 'live' experience.

It is true that in the early stages of a race, TV or S.I.S. shows you far more than you could hope to see on the course unless you had a very powerful telescope. Yet in the vital last two furlongs, recent TV coverage tends to focus in on the first two horses, or even just the winning horse, so that it is very difficult to get an overall picture of the race. At the course, you are in an incomparably better position to judge the race at this stage.

Although watching races on TV is a distinct second best to the 'live' experience, the volume of TV racing, and the availability of video, enables you to practise the art more thoroughly in a relatively short time.

I begin with the simplest question, how to do it.

Before the race starts, try and memorise as many of the colours as possible. If you watch racing consistently, you will soon learn the colours of the 10 leading owners—such is the concentration of ownership on the Flat at the moment that this knowledge will immediately enable you to identify 1 or 2 colours in almost every race.

Then look for the unfamiliar colours. Unless you have a very good memory for colour, take some short cuts. Make a note of the colours of the caps, as at a distance these are easy to pick out. Choose first of all the striking colours such as white, orange or red—these will be easier to pick out at a distance.

Next look for distinctive characteristics exhibited by the horses—the greys, the white socks, those with bandaged feet, or those with a white bridle or noseband. Without much difficulty you should now have easily identified about 6 horses.

Televised races are invaluable for learning the colours—beginning with fields of 8 to 12 runners, watch a few races, non-handicaps or handicaps, in which you have no financial interest, with the sound turned town, until you learn this basic skill.

Beyond learning to pick out about 6 easily identified horses in each race, I think that unless you are a Peter O'Sullevan, who can memorise fields of 35 and more runners, you should be content with knowing at most 4 more horses in each race. At any rate, you should make sure that you know the colours of *all* the horses of a certain type—those you think are about to strike form, previous winners of handicaps (especially those which are carrying a penalty), and horses you may have noted previously.

Now you have learned the colours for the race, if you are watching the race at the course, you should consider carefully where to go.

The ideal position is, of course, as high up as possible so that you can get a panoramic view of the last two furlongs. The best courses for this (in order) are: York, Ascot, Sandown and Newmarket. However high you can get above the racing, the obvious place to go would seem to be opposite the winning post, but I don't think that this is in fact the best position.

Personally I favour a position about 1f–2f down the course—this is where many jockeys ask their horses the crucial question. In the words of the founder of modern handicapping, Admiral Rous: '...his (the handicapper's) station should be at the distance-post, where horses are pulled, not at the winning-post, where they are extended.' (*On the Laws and Practice of Horse Racing* 1850 p124).

Unlike the Admiral, we are not looking for dishonest practice, but it is at the same position, the 'distance' (240 yards from the finish) that the race is frequently won or lost—those horses which cannot go the distance drop out, and those which are about to make a final challenge begin to make their run to the finish.

Finally, to watch the race you need a good pair of 8 × 50 binoculars—they can be heavy to carry about, but it's worth it. The modern lightweight kind often have a higher magnification, but a narrower field of vision, whereas we are aiming to keep as much of the field in view as possible.

I never watch a race all the way through with binoculars. In the final stages of the race, you should rely on the unaided eye, scanning as much of the field as possible. At this stage, binoculars tend to restrict the field of vision too much.

I have always thought that it is much easier to 'read' races on courses with an uphill finish, because the result is generally much more clear-cut. In the last 2 furlongs, tired horses roll and leave plenty of gaps for the strong finisher. At this point, the field is usually fairly compact, but not in that packed formation which gives rise to so many 'hard luck' stories. Reading the race reports of several commentators, it seems that this is the general opinion. By contrast, race reports from flat or downhill-finish courses seem to be much more cautious and less clear-cut. It is a good idea, therefore, to start practising race-reading at the courses with an uphill finish: of these, the best view is to be had at Ascot, Newmarket, Salisbury and Sandown.

Now having settled the preliminary questions, let us tackle the main question—what are we to look for?

The natural inclination of most punters is, understandably enough, to keep their eyes glued on the horse which they have backed, to the exclusion of all the others. Once its chance of winning has gone they lose interest in the race and do not watch their 'own' horse again, whereas the experienced race reader knows that there is as much to be learned from watching the beaten horses. Even when it is clear that your horse is going to win, watch the race carefully right through to the end—and afterwards.

Try and make your race reading parallel the effort put in by the jockeys during

27

the race—alertness at the beginning; keeping in touch for the early and middle stages of the race; and maximum concentration in the last two furlongs.

To the uninitiated, a 6f sprint seems to be 'all over in a minute'—but even at this distance, it is possible to learn a great deal by watching the race carefully. I will now review an imaginary race over 6 furlongs at Newmarket to show the wealth of information you can gather by doing so.

Just before the off, remind yourself of what you are trying to do—you are aiming to assess not only the performance of individual horses, but also the reliability of the race as a whole as a yardstick for future races. Now let us look at the race stage by stage.

Going down to post. Even the most experienced judge of a horse can learn more from watching horses going down to post than from paddock inspection. The ideal type of action is free, flowing and relaxed, which enables a horse to cope with most types of going and to reserve his energy for the race. It is not necessarily a bad sign, however, if a horse fights for his head when cantering down: he may have done this in the past and still been able to win (here the previous record contained in *Raceform Note-Book* must be consulted). Horses with a 'round' action usually prefer soft going, while the 'sharp' actioned types like to bounce off the firmer ground.

The horses leave the stalls. It is not always a disadvantage, even in sprints, to leave the stalls slowly. For example, on courses which have a stiff uphill finish, like Newmarket or Ascot, there is plenty of time to recover lost ground. Older horses which have retained their finishing speed are often slowly away but flying at the finish (eg YOUNG INCA 1987).

It is quite a different matter on the easier courses, or races which begin downhill (eg Epsom). The sprint races are then often won or lost as the stalls open, when the quick starters can gain an unassailable lead.

Be careful of 'hard luck' stories here—the horse which loses a great deal of ground at the start, but runs on well at the finish without winning. This horse may have done so before, and it's quite possible that if he did get a good start he would have nothing in reserve for the last furlong.

The first furlong. Here you should look for the following points.

Firstly, what is the early pace like? If it is slow, and where there is an obvious reluctance by any of the runners to set the pace, you should view the eventual result of the race with considerable scepticism. A slow early pace notoriously produces misleading results. **Pace makes the race.**

On the other hand, it is not always easy to judge the pace by eye. What one really needs is sectional timing, ie the time recorded at the end of the first two furlongs. In American racing, where times are much more significant, it is standard practice to time each quarter furlong. Unfortunately, it is unlikely that this will be introduced here, as there seems to be little general demand for it.

Secondly, if the early pace is good, which of the runners are being taken off their feet, struggling to go the pace? This is one of the surest signs that a horse is running out of its class. A horse which jumps from, say, a 0–90 to a 0–110, is much more likely to be left for dead in the early stages of the race than it is to remain in contention but be outpaced at the finish.

This is also the moment of truth for horses which have won a non-handicap in great style—but in truth in the earlier race there was nothing to beat. They are literally run off their feet in the early stages and use up all their speed just staying in touch.

The next two furlongs. On a straight course like Newmarket, it is often difficult to know which side of the field is in the lead. You may be able to find landmarks

28

on the other side of the course to give you a clue—the most difficult place for reading the early stages of a race is Newmarket, as there are very few 'markers' on the great bare expanses of open heathland.

In most races a lightly-weighted horse or a horse with a poor chance will hare off in front, and still be several lengths clear about half-way through the race. Don't make the mistake of focussing on this horse—keep it in the corner of your eye and watch the others as in 9 races out of 10 the early pacemaker will come back to the field.

What is happening behind the pacemaker? Here a knowledge of different jockeys' riding style is invaluable. It used to be said of Sir Gordon Richards that if you saw him sitting perfectly still with about 3 furlongs to go, you knew you had lost your money, as he was trying to conserve the energy of a horse which did not have much left. Conversely, if you saw Lester Piggott doing exactly the same thing, you knew that you were in with a very good chance, as he was sitting there with a horse ready to go. If you see a jockey like Carson who generally relies on a driving finish through the last two furlongs begin to drive his horse at this point, about 3 furlongs out, you can be fairly certain that the horse is losing touch.

Thus the questions which a knowledge of a jockey's racing style can help you resolve are: does the jockey have the proverbial 'double handful' or is his mount beginning to tire? is the horse running much too freely, fighting for his head and wasting energy which should have been conserved for the finish? is the horse being 'held up' at the rear of the field?—this can be a very good sign, as it means that a horse may be capable of a strong late finish.

When the race is over, look back at your notes on this stage of the race. Would a particular horse have had a better chance if he had been ridden in a different way—for example, would it have been better if a horse which have been given his head had been 'held up'?

If a fancied horse which has kept up with the pace, although not necessarily among the leaders, begins to fade badly at this point, this often means that his running is too bad to be true—he may have the virus, or have injured himself during the course of the race.

This stage in the race is one of the most fruitful sources of 'hard luck' stories, but I always regard such stories with considerable scepticism. If the horse is ridden by a good jockey, then the fault may lie with the horse, that is, it makes its own 'hard luck'. If it runs on strongly at the finish this may be quite misleading—if it had been shown daylight earlier in the race, then it would probably have faded and finished down the field. I would only consider such 'hard luck' stories if the horse had a proven ability to win races.

Even if a horse wins after being baulked or failing to find an opening at this stage, be wary of concluding that he would have won much more easily if he had had a clear run. Many horses lose interest when they are not 'covered up'—the moment they see daylight in front of them they seem to slow down. This is not because they are not genuine—such horses will often show great resolution in a driving finish when they have other horses near them.

At Newmarket and other courses with an uphill finish, there is plenty of opportunity for a clear run on the final hill as tired horses roll and leave exploitable openings, so in our race we are far less likely to see any 'hard luck' stories than at other courses, such as Chester or Epsom (see ch 6), where such openings are much less likely to occur.

I am equally inclined to be sceptical about the winner of a race in which there was a considerable amount of scrimmaging behind. In this case it makes much more sense to rate this an unreliable race rather than speculate about the future chances of those involved in the scrimmaging.

The final three furlongs. This is where you should apply maximum concentration. In the preceding two furlongs, it was difficult to retain your concentration, especially on the long straight courses such as Newmarket where you cannot see very much until this point.

In most races, the field begins to bunch together again from about 3 furlongs out. Sometimes, however, the front runner continues to gallop on, making all to the winning post. This type of winner is often very difficult to evaluate.

In some cases, he may have simply 'slipped his field', as the other jockeys realise too late that he has gained an irretrievable advantage. If you think that this is what has happened, then it would be unwise to back this horse next time out. In the next race, if he does not seize the early lead, he will be done for; if he does, the other jockeys will now be wise to this ploy and will challenge him before he can set up a long lead.

This is a difficult judgement to make—the only way you can make it easier is by watching the horses behind the leader. If their jockeys are beginning to roust their horses along at the three furlong mark, then clearly the front-runner has them all in trouble—this is a good sign. If not, then he may simply have taken them all by surprise.

The rarest case of all is where the jockey 'waits in front' letting the field come back to him a few lengths, then lengthening the distance again. This takes jockeyship of a very high order indeed—the best case I can remember (although not in a handicap) was Lester Piggott's riding of COMMANCHE RUN in the 1984 St. Leger. It is quite possible to ride this kind of race in a sprint.

From this point, most races finish in two ways: a horse emerges from the pack sets up a lead of 2 or 3 lengths and holds it to the line; or there is a driving finish right up to the line, with perhaps 2 lengths covering the first 6 horses home.

In the first case, **it is important to observe the horses within 4 lengths of the eventual winner.** Are they being ridden out—are they eased with some way to go? This kind of result must not be interpreted too literally—if the winner has the field well strung out behind him after winning in this way, his victory may not be very significant. In fact, this kind of race is most common either early in the season, when perhaps half the field is unfit, or on very soft–heavy going, when many of the runners will simply be unable to act on the going.

Also be sceptical about the chances of a horse which is noted as 'running on well at the finish' in this kind of race. He may be doing so precisely because he is not under any kind of pressure—this is a classic case of flattering to deceive.

The second type of finish (when several horses are ridden out to the line and the result is in doubt to the last moment), is very helpful to the handicapper. **You can be fairly certain that this will be a reliable result which can be used for checking handicap ratings.**

The horses which will have been ridden up to the line fall into two categories. In the first type, they may be conceding a great deal of weight or carrying a penalty for a recent win. If he is of good enough class, he will be able to go the early pace, but will struggle in the closing stages—the distinction is important for future reference.

The horse which carries a penalty and is in touch at this stage, runs genuinely but cannot find enough to win, being anchored by the extra weight. This sort of performance is a godsend to the handicapper. It means that the horse has run up to the limit of his previous performance and can therefore operate as a benchmark for the other horses; and it also establishes what the present limit is for this horse.

Thus if a horse is on the 80 mark, improves to 84, then carries a 7 lbs penalty, bringing him up to 87, but runs to 84, it means that 84 is his mark. Sometimes this horse may come out again on this mark, and should be considered.

Secondly, a horse may be genuine enough, but lack the sparkle to win, setting up a sequence of seconds and thirds. Very infrequently they do win, this appearing to justify the newspaper comment about these horses: 'His turn is near' 'Should be winning soon.' **I love to read these phrases—such comments can often create a false price about these horses which we can take advantage of to back another runner.**

Genuine horses of this kind, however, are very useful for providing a yardstick for the handicapper. However, for the future, they do not give the private handicapper any advantages. The official handicapper will probably come to exactly the same conclusions as you do—which means that you won't have anything 'in hand'.

However, there is one more, much rarer type of finish—the best of all for the private handicapper—the horse with a 'turn of foot' which can produce a strong late run to snatch the race virtually on the line.

In all fairness, the official handicapper can hardly be too harsh on a horse which wins in this style only by a neck or a head, but if you think that the horse had much more in hand, then you have a potential goldmine. There aren't many of these horses around—perhaps no more than 15 new ones emerge each season at the leading racecourses but once you have identified them they can win two or even three more races before the handicapper catches up with them.

It's even better news if they win a sprint in this way—horses can retain this burst of finishing speed until they are 9 or 10 years old. The handicapper is bound to catch up with them in the space of one season (say when they are 5 years old) but after one season of their running unplaced on their new mark, they are gradually dropped down the handicap scale again to their winning mark, when they can produce that devastating burst of acceleration once again (eg YOUNG INCA 1987).

However, a word of caution. You must be fairly confident that overall this was a truly-run race. A horse which comes off the pace with a strong late burst at the end of a slowly-run race may give a most misleading impression of his true abilities. It is not always possible to judge pace by eye—the only reliable indicator is the speed figure, recorded in *Raceform Handicap Book*. A good example of this was the performance of TAKENHALL in a sprint handicap over six furlongs at Newmarket, in 1988. Nearer last than first with a furlong to go, he came with a tremendous late run to get up on the line. However, the speed figure (45) showed that this was not quite such a devastating performance—evidently, the slow pace of the race had enabled him to sprint clear from some slow horses in the final stages.

After the winning post. Some horses show considerable zest when it's all over—do not be misled into thinking that with a slightly longer race, they might have won. Unless their style of running earlier in the race suggests that this might be the case, it is easy to run on well after the race is over, and when the other runners do not provide any opposition.

However, if you have seen a horse win with a late finish, it is an extra bonus to see that he continues to run on so strongly that the jockey has difficulty in pulling him up.

Be patient when watching races—if you haven't seen a late flyer for several weeks, it is easy to think that they are a dying breed. It is a common mistake in this period even with very experienced race-readers to that think they will never see another horse of this type—and then they might see two in one afternoon! **As in every other aspect of handicap racing, you must be patient but always on the alert.**

CHAPTER FIVE

How to Use a Private Handicap

How can you use a private handicap to find winners?

If you follow blindly the top two or any private handicaps or rating systems you will have a success rate of about 30%; the top four will include about 65% of the winners. I have checked the leading systems and the difference between their success rates over a period of time is minimal.

However, even if you aim to bet in every handicap you can improve that success rate to about 40%, if you carefully consider the following factors: weight; class; recent form; sex; key races; going; distance; size of field; draw . It is easiest to do so by analysing an example.

GOODWOOD 10f handicap (0–115)

VIRGINIA	3–9–10 (inc 7x)	+ 1	(filly)
CHARLES	8–9–0 (inc 7x)	− 1	(8 year old gelding)
FIONA	3–7–7	− 2	

Weight

As I have said before, this is the biggest area of confusion in punters' minds. They would look at this handicap, see that VIRGINIA is set to carry 9–10 and say that she has too much weight. Perhaps in an earlier race in a lower grade FIONA has been carrying, say 9–0, and the punter would now say that her task is easier as she has gone down in the weights.

But in our opinion it is VIRGINIA who is 'well in' at the weights, so that relative to other horses she is not carrying too much. But in carrying 9st 10lbs is she carrying too much in *absolute* terms? This depends on a number of factors.

Say that in a given race, two horses are both on the same handicap mark, and, in our opinion correctly rated—and are to carry a high weight. One is a small, light-framed horse; the other a big, well-built horse. The answer is obvious—but the official handicapper cannot take physical differences between horses into account. Interestingly enough, until Admiral Rous's period, in certain races horses *were* allocated weight in relation to their size.There are exceptions, but the big, well-built horse is clearly more suited to carrying great lumps of weight. Never back a small horse to do so, unless he has already shown himself capable of carrying the weight.

But the amount of weight carried can have other less obvious effects. On some courses, races are run over straight, flat or uphill tracks (for example, York or Newmarket) and they go at a tremendous gallop; on others they run on the turn (Chester) or on an undulating track which does not allow a full gallop, until the last finishing section (for example, Brighton or Epsom). In the latter case, horses carrying a heavy weight are not at such a disadvantage. Chapter 6 tells you at which tracks top weights have a good record.

A useful old saying which I have found to be true far more often than not is: '*A horse can give away weight but not distance*'. Say that in their previous race CHARLES beat FIONA by a length, but is now carrying a 7lbs penalty ie on a strict reading of 1 lb for the 1 length beating, CHARLES is now 6 lbs worse off.

One bet you can be certain of—the newspapers will say: 'should reverse the form on more favourable terms'. This is where your judgement comes in. Either from your own observation or from racecourse reports, you may have noted that FIONA was 'held' by the winner, and unless there is a very drastic alteration of the weights (of the order of a stone or more) CHARLES will win again. In my experience, this happens far more often than the form is reversed.

Perhaps this happens not only for the reason suggested but also because of the psychological aspect. The onus is on the jockey of the second horse to reverse the placings, whereas the jockey of the previous winner has the incalculable asset of confidence in his mount.

Apart from this, what are we to make of the effect of the penalty? In principle a 7 lbs penalty is the same as raising the mark by 7. I say ' in principle' because the records show that penalised horses have a very poor record on certain courses—for example, sprint races at Ascot. This also applies to certain races—a winner of the Portland Handicap at the Doncaster St. Leger rarely carries a penalty to victory in the Ayr Gold Cup (see the details given under each course, ch 6).

One final point on penalties. The effect of the additional weight can be offset if a good claiming apprentice is engaged—of course, this is particularly significant if last time out the selection was ridden by an ordinary jockey.

Class

This is also related to weight. A horse engaged in two handicaps of different grades may be set to carry 18lbs less in one handicap whereas his handicap mark has not changed. This is one of the most common fallacies among punters, and perpetuated by journalists. How often do you hear or read 'So-and-so has a good chance, as he's gone down x lbs in the weights.'

Having less weight to carry will often not make the horse run any faster, although having more weight may slow him down. A horse which is carrying significantly less weight has usually been raised in class—if there is a dramatic jump in class and finds himself out of his class, he will usually be outpaced early on. Some horses are able to win while giving away great lumps of weight while running in lower grade races, but when running with a light weight in a higher grade are outclassed (for example, GOUVERNO 1984).

How do we resolve this problem? A horse could win a lowly handicap in excellent style early in the season and in our book be well in hand in relation to the official handicap. His over-optimistic owner then enters him for a handicap at Royal Ascot—with predictable results. But strictly on the book he will show up as a good chance.

My general principles are as follows:

Firstly, I do not bet in 0–75 handicaps, nor do I consider any form from such races, as the jump to a higher class is usually too great. The only exception to this is the Epsom Derby meeting, where, exceptionally, horses which have previously won 0–75 races seem to be able to make the transition to higher grades (eg KIOWA 1983; FIRST DIVISION 1986).

Secondly, I prefer to back a horse which is running in the same grade or the one just above it: for example, **going from a 0–90 to a 0–100 is well within reach, but if your selection is entered for a 0–110, you have to be fairly confident about its chance.**

Thirdly, although they are theoretically the same, the same grade of handicap at different racecourses seems to attract a different class of runner. Thus, in my view, a 0–90 at Wolverhampton is of a lower class than a 0–90 at Sandown. This is especially important during the high season, from mid-June to the end of September.

With apologies to the racecourse authorities concerned, I have grouped all Britain's racecourses according to the class and form value of their handicap racing. My classification has no bearing on stakes or Classics (that is, if the reader has ignored everything I have said and is still interested in that category of racing!). For example, the Chester May meeting which I consider a Class Two is indisputably a Class One meeting as far as non-handicap racing is concerned.

This *class value* is not based on the level of prize money but on my experience of the actual competitiveness of the races themselves, ie the class of the form it takes to win at these meetings. As you will see, it is quite close to the official classification.

CLASS ONE: Ascot Ayr (Western Meeting only) Doncaster (St. Leger Meeting only) Epsom (Derby Meeting only) Goodwood (July meeting only) Newbury Newmarket Sandown York

CLASS TWO: Ayr (other meetings) Brighton Chester (May meeting) Doncaster (other meetings) Goodwood (other meetings) Haydock Kempton Leicester Lingfield Newcastle Salisbury

CLASS THREE: Bath Beverley Chepstow Chester (other meetings) Epsom (other meetings) Nottingham Pontefract Redcar Ripon Thirsk Windsor Wolverhampton Yarmouth

CLASS FOUR Carlisle Edinburgh Folkestone Hamilton Warwick

Some races I consider Class One, at courses otherwise of lower grade, for example the Great St. Wilfrid Handicap at Ripon, and these are dealt with in chapter 6.

The *form value* is my assessment of how reliable is the form produced at different courses. It diverges quite noticeably from the *class value* and the official classifications. Such classifications owe quite a good deal to personal opinion, and I urge the reader to make his own classification, based of course on a study of the form book.

This is my classification of form value (in descending order):

CLASS ONE Royal Ascot Newmarket Sandown Salisbury Ascot (other meetings) Leicester Newcastle Haydock (up to 7f 40y) Hamilton Bath Doncaster York

All the courses which are Class One for form value produce very reliable form, because of the nature of the courses (see ch 6). With the exception of Doncaster and York, all these courses have an uphill finish. Such courses provide a true test of a racehorse—races tend to be truly run and rarely produce misleading results. I have ranked them in rough order of reliability. The reader may be surprised to see Bath, Hamilton, Leicester and Salisbury in this class, and Goodwood in Class Two, but although racing is invariably of a higher quality at the latter course, it is not as testing a course as the other four.

CLASS TWO Goodwood Kempton Redcar Nottingham Ripon Thirsk Lingfield

These courses produce reliable form, but the courses in the Class One *form value* classifications have a distinct edge.

CLASS THREE Beverley Brighton Chepstow Epsom Haydock (over 7f 40f) Newbury Pontefract Wolverhampton Yarmouth

Because of their peculiar configuration, the form produced at these courses *cannot* be reliably taken to other courses. With the exception of Epsom, I think that a previous course and distance win is *essential* if you considering betting at these courses.

CLASS FOUR Chester

In a class of its own, because even a previous course and distance winner is likely to find trouble during running because of the tight turns and short finishing section.

Recent Form

Nearly all my selections are based on improving horses with good recent form—ideally with winning form or running well within the last 28 days. If you back a horse which won last time out, there are no 'ifs and buts' about its recent record, no scrutinising a 'promising' run into 6th place in the hope that the horse *may* be able to reproduce its form of a now somewhat distant past.

On the other hand, it is sometimes difficult to decide what to do if a horse has shown this good (winning) form some time ago. I think it is a good rule to be very wary if the horse has not been on a racecourse for the last 28 days—this is especially true in the early (before the Epsom Derby) and late (after the Ayr Western Meeting) stages of the season.

Conversely, a horse *can* be brought out too soon after a hard race—this is especially true of winners of hard fought races at the Royal Ascot meeting.

Here I do consider it useful to study the past record of the trainer, to find out whether he is able to keep a horse fit but only produce him ready to win at fairly lengthy intervals (eg 2 months).

However, don't confine yourself to the most recent race. Look back through the handicap marks for the current season, to see if the horse is considered to be making steady improvement. In this race, VIRGINIA stands out as having won last time out and her handicap mark showed a steady improvement from the beginning of the season. 3 year olds in particular can make extraordinary improvement (eg MOON MADNESS 1986—see ch 10).

Unless there is good reason to do so, I take the mark gained on recent form as being the most indicative. With the benefit of hindsight, it is always possible to go back through the form and find that the winner did record a higher mark at some point on the past.

The only good reason to look back over more than a few weeks is when assessing a handicap run on a specialists' course (eg Sandown 5f), to see what mark the horse ran to when last performing on this course (but in the same season only). Also, some horses run several pounds better at certain courses than others. I am not sure whether the official handicapper can in all fairness take this fully into account.

For instance, in 1987 EVER SHARP ran at Ascot on 23 September (Race 2961: 6f 0–110), where he had previously won on 20 June (Race 1233: 5f 0–115). In between these two races he had run honestly but slightly out of contention. Thus I had downgraded him a few pounds—his mark from the earlier Ascot race was higher than his current mark.

Unless a horse has run so badly in his intervening races as to suggest that he is not holding his form, then earlier form even 3 months old should be considered. This only applies if it is clear that the horse does have a preference for the course, and is most likely to occur at the 'specialist' courses, such as Ascot or Epsom. Thus, another example from 1987 was CLANTIME.

36

Sex

Fillies can make spectacular improvement in a very short time—perhaps more than any other type of horse. This tends to happen later in the season, particularly when they get the sun on their backs, from August onwards. If you must back a filly, it is usually best to wait until the after the July Goodwood meeting before backing it to do so. **Therefore I find it a good rule to back fillies only after the July Goodwood meeting, as they often show spectacular improvement from this point onwards.**

Nevertheless, at any time of the season, you must always inspect a filly in the paddock before placing a bet. Fillies tend to 'go' in their coat very suddenly ie their coat becomes dull, even matted. This is a very reliable indicator that a filly will not run up to her best form.

At the other end of the scale of equine reliability are geldings. One of the best trainers ever for placing handicappers, the late R J Colling, once said: 'If I had a stable full of geldings, I'd get the bookmakers on the run.' Geldings are very reliable, tough and consistent and from my own records are the best bet of all. Even if driven out to win, they can be relied on to win again (which I wouldn't do with a colt which had had to be driven out). If you fancy a gelding's chances, it's worth increasing your stakes. Alternatively, if you wanted to be very selective, you would bet only on geldings.

Some colts which have ability clearly have their minds on activities more interesting than racing. After all you can't blame them for not knowing that they have to put their time in on their racecourse before they can go to the stud farm!

From our point of view, they might improve considerably as geldings. A horse may be gelded relatively late in his career, and it is always worth noting any improvement which follows such an operation. However, the operation does not *always* make a better racehorse—bad luck for the connections (and even more for the horse) who now have the worst of both worlds.

It is much more common to find sprint handicappers as geldings, as they are often unfashionably bred and have little stud value. In Flat racing terms, they seem to be able to go on for ever—in recent years, for example, BRI-EDEN (1983) and YOUNG INCA (1989) won top class handicaps as 11 year olds, perhaps the equivalent of a 45 year old human athlete.

Age

Should we be put off by the fact that CHARLES is an 'aged' horse, that is, older than 6 years? As this is a race of 7 furlongs of more, I would be extremely reluctant to consider his chance. As a general rule, aged horses only win races over a distance at the beginning of the season, when some races are not very competitive. Sprint handicappers can win valuable handicaps even at the age of 9 (in 1987 DAWN'S DELIGHT won the valuable Portland Handicap at Doncaster; YOUNG INCA won races at Ascot and Goodwood).

At the other end of the scale, what chance does VIRGINIA have as a 3 year old running against older horses? Although the weight-for-age scale theoretically gives 3 year olds a chance against their elders from the beginning of the season, they are not really in with a chance until after the Royal Ascot meeting. Before then, I would not back a 3 year old to beat an older horse unless it had *already* done so.

One point about age which should always be considered. The official birthday of all horses is 1 January, which may be significantly different from their real age.

In a 3 year old race in May, therefore, one horse may be 3 years exactly (having been born in May) and another 3y 4m—quite a marked difference at this stage of their development.

Key Races

Is the horse good enough to win this particular race? Here you should look at chapter 6. If, for example, this race was being run at Ascot, then you would rule out VIRGINIA as the records show that penalised horses run very badly on this course; and also that it is essential to have won previously over course and distance.

On the other hand, if the race was run at, say, Newmarket, the records of this race might show that Ascot winners or winners last time out at other courses have a good chance.

Going

In my view, this is the most significant factor in causing shock results. The problem is not so acute when the going is consistently of one type, either good or soft. Then you can simply check back through the form book to see what conditions favour your selection. Some horses have a clear record of preferring a particular type of going. But what do you do when your selection has to run on a type of going he has not encountered before?

For example, if the horse is now to run on soft going, and previously has only run on good going? There is no theoretical answer to this question—you have to be at the course to watch your selection go down to post. If he shows any signs of a 'high' or 'sharp' action, then he is unlikely to act on the going.

If you cannot get to the course but are prepared to take a chance, then unless the going is likely to be extreme (fast or heavy) you can ignore any changes. This also depends on the course: even minor changes in the going seem to have a much more marked effect at some courses (particularly York) than others (Newmarket): see chapter 6 for full details.

It is the extremes of going (fast or heavy) which cause the problems—in these cases you must have evidence of previous ability to act on these extremes.

Serious problems arise when the going changes fairly quickly from one type to the other, as it does in some seasons (eg 1987)—if the weather is consistently wet or dry, then at least you know what to expect. Naturally, such rapid changes are most likely to happen in the spring or the autumn, and constitute an additional reason for avoiding this period.

If you cannot get to the course to judge for yourself, it is essential to try to get the most up-to-date reports on the going. Unfortunately, it has to be said that the going reports issued by the courses are frequently unreliable. For example, on the first 2 days of the York August meeting in 1988, the going was said to be no faster than 'good to firm', yet several course records were broken.

It would be a great help to the backer if the Jockey Club were to adopt the French system of measuring the state of the going using a 'penetrometer'. This is like the common garden tool about 30 cms long and made of metal, which is used for measuring moisture.

Distance

This is far less of a problem than going, as horses are usually run over a suitable distance—and the few exceptions seem to follow certain rules. An improving 3 year old is often asked to step up in distance, say from 8f to 10f. He is usually capable of doing so, and I cannot think of a case where defeat in these circumstances was due to the extra distance.

The more difficult case, I find, is where a good winner at, say, 8f is put back to 7f. It is more difficult to judge from the style of running over the longer distance whether the horse will have sufficient speed to win over the shorter. Here Key Races can sometimes be of advantage—eg the winner of the 8f **Royal Hunt Cup** at Ascot can be successfully put back to the 7f of the **Bunbury Cup** at Newmarket and still win.

The most clear-cut distance is 7f, very much a specialists' distance. Winners have to have enough speed to win at 6f and enough stamina to stay 8f. A good 7f horse is a real goldmine, and can be relied on over this distance (TREMBLANT 1985; ARADU, GOLD MINORIES 1988). 7f is the only distance over which a previous distance win is essential.

Distance must also be considered in relation to course layout. Sometimes it is said that a winner over 6f on a flat course, such as Doncaster or Kempton, will be able to act on a stiff 5f course, such as Ascot or Sandown, but this is rarely the case and it is unwise to bet on such reasoning.

Draw

For all races, the runners are allocated by draw to their places in the starting stalls, with '1' on the left hand side as you look up the course from the stalls. It depends, therefore, upon whether the course is left-handed or right-handed, as to whether '1' is to run along the inside or out the outside rail.

On most courses, and especially in the longer races (more than 8f) the draw is not of any great consequence. But in a few cases, it is of very great significance. The information is given in chapter 6.

The reader may now be asking: how on earth can I compile a private handicap and check through all the factors listed above for every handicap race, without spending so much time that I have to give up my job?

The answer is—you can't, unless you specialise. To compile a rating for every handicap race, and to check every handicap is simply not possible for someone who works full-time. There are about 1500 handicaps each Flat season so it is clearly out of the question.

How should you specialise? You can specialise in a certain type of handicap. It is probably best to follow sprint handicaps only, as there is plenty of form from previous seasons. There are about 320 of these each year, of which just over half are graded higher than 0–75.

Or you could concentrate on certain racecourses. I concentrate on the southern racecourses, because I can travel easily to most of them. But you could easily work out a 'Midlands circuit', a 'Northern circuit' or a 'Scottish circuit' depending on where you live.

I also concentrate on handicaps from 0–90 upwards. Here, followers of the 'southern circuit' are better off than anywhere else in the country. Occasionally I will consider form from a 0–75 in the early part of the season, but only if the horse is rated 50 upwards. Otherwise you are dealing with the lower end of the racing talent—and the higher the class of horse the more consistent he tends to be.

I also consider all distances up to 12f, and mainly concentrate on the high season, from the Royal Ascot meeting to the Ayr Western meeting, and thereafter only on the Ascot, Newmarket and York meetings. This means considering about 100 handicaps per season—a much more manageable number. **Even then, I do not attempt to find the winner of every race. In my view the best way to use a private handicap is not to think of finding a selection for every race, but to identify improving horses which you think have a pound or two in hand for future handicaps, to try to anticipate which races they should be aimed at.**

Don't try and second-guess what the trainer *will* do but try to work out what would be best for the horse. If the two don't coincide, don't be swayed by the fact that he is a leading/well-known trainer. Thus if you think that your winner would be best aimed at a Newmarket 6f with a penalty but should be avoided if he ran at Ascot with a penalty this prepares you for your decision on the day.

If the improvement appears to be mainly confined to the most recent race, go back through the form book even to the beginning of the horse's career to see if you can find a possible reason. Perhaps he has never run over this trip before—occasionally a horse may find his right trip quite late in his career; perhaps he has not been ridden like this before—if he has usually been ridden up with the pace but now comes to win from off the pace, this is a very good sign.

Keep this record up to date and with sprinters keep it over a number of years—it will pay off over quite a long period. For example, I backed YOUNG INCA in 1987 relying on my notes of his performance in 1985 and previous years.

Size of Field

At one end of the scale, I have found it good policy never to take form from a race of less than 6 runners nor to bet in such a race. Such races often give a false result, because they are not run at a true pace. Far more often than not, a small field means a slow pace over the first few furlongs and a two furlong sprint to the finish. Furthermore, the type of horse which, although perfectly genuine, needs to be 'covered up' to produce a good late run has very little chance of doing so—usually, he will see daylight far too early in the race and be unable to give of his best.

I don't find big fields (say, over 15 runners) such a problem. The larger the field, the more likely it is that the race will be run at a cracking pace. The danger with a large field, is of course, that your selection will get 'boxed in' and will be unable to get a clear run. In this case it depends on the type of course (see ch 6). On a big wide course with an uphill finish at the end of a strongly run race there are plenty of gaps opening up at the end of a race as the beaten horses run off a true line. On a flat or down hill course the danger of getting 'boxed in' in a large field is much greater. Perhaps the two courses where betting in large fields involves the greatest risk are Chester and Epsom.

Now you have made your selection, how do you go about backing it?

On the Day

When you go to the course or the betting shop, you should go with the intention of backing a *particular* horse (s) at a *suitable* price (see ch 8). How often do you see people looking through the sporting press or even the form book on the way to the racecourse, or even when they have arrived, trying to make up their minds there and then? A soldier does not go into battle still reading his basic training manual!

You have to be prepared in every way, even down to what you wear—you should dress sensibly and inconspicuously.

Sensibly, because you may walk up to four miles while you are on some courses—if it is a new course to you, you should walk around as much of it as possible. No amount of description in this or any other book can make up for your own first-hand observation.

Inconspicuously, because you are expecting to make money. Even if you bet on credit, so that no cash changes hands, if you are dressed up to play the part of the 'great gambler', you will attract attention from some undesirable who may be waiting for you in the carpark when you go home. The only person's attention you want to attract is that of the bookmaker when you are placing your bet.

Give yourself plenty of time at the course—especially if it's new to you and you need to familiarise yourself with its layout. If for whatever reason you find it a bit of a rush to get from the paddock to a good viewing position (for example, at Epsom it is an awkward journey) concentrate on race-reading of the races in which you are not involved, and save your energy for 'your' race.

You should plan a routine for watching races: inspection in the paddock; watching the runners down to the start; placing your bet; and watching the race from a suitable vantage point. It's amazing how few racegoers do this in a systematic way—but you cannot hope to win without doing so. To do this properly for every race, you could easily cover 2 or 3 miles at a big track—so you have to be fit.

In the paddock. Here, you are not looking at conformation or how the horse walks from the point of view of finding a future classic winner. All you need to know is: does the horse look fit? does he look relaxed? The signs of fitness are: a gleaming coat, ears pricked, eyes alert and a springy walk. If any of these are missing, or if the horse looks 'sour', plodding around listlessly with no apparent interest in his surroundings, then *don't bet.*

Many animals lose their chance in the paddock by sweating up and using the energy they should have saved for the race. This applies particularly to fillies and the younger colts. On the other hand, some horses go down to the post absolutely dripping with sweat—and still win, which they may have done before. You need to look this up in a form guide—*Raceform Note-Book* is particularly informative on this point.

Down to the post. However relaxed yet alert a horse may look in the paddock, it is only when he gets into his paces that you can form a reliable impression of his action. It is then much simpler to differentiate the big long-striding types from the close-coupled horses with a shorter action. The former are probably unsuited by sharp or downhill courses, while the latter may find it easier to accelerate quickly, so as to be able to win on courses with an uphill finish.

Concentrate on your selection as it goes down to post, but also try to make notes on as many other horses as possible—you never know when these notes will come in handy. Look for a relaxed flowing action—if a horse fights for his head all the way down to the post, he may expend too much energy before the race starts. He may appear ill at ease on the going—when the going is soft, look for a 'round' action, when it is fast, for a 'sharp' action. If you see what you think are bad signs, check your notes on his previous races—he may have gone down fighting for his head all the way in his last race, and still have won. If you see an action which he has not shown in previous races, then *don't bet.*

Placing your bet. Now concentrate on what you have come for—and don't change your mind on the basis of what you may hear other people say. Of course, you may decide *not* to back your selection, if it is unfit or sweating; or goes down to the post badly; or the jockey puts up a large amount of overweight; or the going has changed to the disadvantage of your horse. That is why you should go to the course, as you can't see these things for yourself at home. You should not bet before you have made certain that none of the last-minute hitches just mentioned are likely to affect the horse's chances.

Increasingly, credit bookmakers and betting shops offer 'early prices' on the morning of the race. Sometimes you will find that you could have got, say, 4–1, in the morning, and cannot do better than 5–2 on the course—and you may have 'missed' a 4–1 winner.

But however 'good' the price, you are betting without a full knowledge of the facts—this can only be available just before the race, preferably on the racecourse. Why spend all that time compiling your handicap and then take an unnecessary risk?

Don't change your mind because of what happens in the betting market. You may decide not to bet because you can't get a good enough price about your selection—but don't be put off if it is not favourite or second favourite, if it 'drifts' in the betting.

The worst thing you can do is back a different horse because your horse 'drifts' and another horse seems to be fancied (see ch8 for more on this point). How often do you see punters standing near the bookmakers frenziedly looking through their papers or form books once they see that the betting on a horse opens at an unexpectedly short price, or its price shortens dramatically.

It's even more difficult if you are with a group of friends, when you may feel pressurised to have a bet 'just to be sociable'. Even if you have small bets, just to oblige them, it is amazing how much you can fritter away in the long term doing just this. Invariably, they will know or meet someone on the course, who just happens to be a friend of the uncle of the head lad's brother, and they have some sure-fire information...If you met enough people like this, you would end up with a 'sure-fire' tip for every horse in the race.

Even more so, don't drink. Have you ever seen a bookmaker or any of his employees drinking at the course or in the betting shop? The bookmakers know it would be the shortest way to Carey Street; and their employees are liable to instant dismissal if caught drinking during working hours.

Watching the race. When you visit a course for the first time, try out several different vantage points. Don't follow the crowd by always standing opposite the winning post, or where there is the largest group of people. The best viewing points are often quite deserted—for example, on top of the stand at Newbury or York. Nor is it always necessary to go into the Members' Enclosure to get the best view—many punters go there simply for snobbish reasons. For example, at Salisbury the view from the Tattersalls stand is far better than the view from the Members' Enclosure.

The golden rules must be:

Make your basic decision before you go to the course;

Only change your mind about your selection on the basis of what you have seen, and not because of the betting market;

Go by yourself, unless you can find someone else who shares your serious approach to racing;

Don't drink;

Be selective;

Be patient.

If you get really interested in racing, then you won't find it hard to follow these rules, as you will soon see the point of doing so.

There are two further temptations to deal with, after the race in which your selection was running. If you have backed a winner, it can be tempting to think that your luck is in, so you might as well have a go in the remaining races. It hardly needs emphasising how stupid this is, and in fact this should be a relatively easy course of action to avoid.

What you will find hard to do, and I still find it takes a lot of self-discipline to do, is to keep your morale up when you have a loser and not to give way to depression.

You may have spent two or three hours beforehand studying form, another two or three hours getting to the track—and then your carefully researched selection is well-beaten. The inevitable thought occurs to you: a pin would have been as much use in finding winners!

This is when you must grit your teeth and stick at it. Don't go home in a fit of despondency—stay on the course and watch the remaining races as enthusiastically and carefully as if you had just backed a big winner. It's happened to me more than once that in the next race after I had backed a loser there was a good improving handicapper who more than made up for what I had just lost. If I had given way to dejection and gone home, I would have missed out on a good opportunity. This doesn't mean that I backed it then, but I put it in my notebook for the future.

Finally, to keep you going, remember that *tomorrow is another betting opportunity!*

CHAPTER SIX
Key Races

'Horses for Courses' is an old and true saying, but I wonder how many readers realise that 'Horses for Races' is equally valid, particularly for handicap racing. That is, over the years there is quite a settled pattern about the programme of handicaps such that certain races reliably provide pointers to others.

This is not to say that it is immutable—as certain handicaps lose their value or go out of fashion the pattern changes. For example, the early season handicaps, such as the Newbury Spring Cup or the City and Suburban at Epsom, used to attract much better fields than they do today. However, the pattern does not change rapidly, and can be easily observed when it does.

These 'key races' are much better pointers than, say, two year old races to the Classics, or the Classic trials. As the cumbersome titles bestowed on them by their sponsors change quite frequently I have used the basic name by which they were originally known (eg Victoria Cup).

In this chapter, I point to various key races and crucial information about courses. The reader should keep this record up to date so as to monitor changing patterns. For reasons of space, I have concentrated on the leading races at each course, but you will find that at the big meetings even the lesser races usually follow a pattern. **In a future publication, I will give full details of my analysis of all the major handicaps.**

Ascot

LAYOUT: the 14f round course goes downhill at the start for 3f, then joins the Old Mile on a chute, rises steadily until it joins the Royal Hunt Cup mile with an easy turn about 3f from the finishing point. The last 3f is uphill until about the last 100 yards, which are level.

The Royal Hunt Cup Mile begins with a slight fall for the first furlong, rises to the 5f gate, a slight fall, uphill to the last 100 yards, flat to the finish.

GOING: although the course is set on the Lower Bagshot Sands, it can get waterlogged, and often gets heavy in the spring/autumn. Winners on fast going, however, know that they have had a race, and they make some time to recover.

DRAW: when the going gets soft, high numbers are said to be favoured on the straight course.

Ascot is a very aristocratic racecourse—unless you can get up high in the Members' Grandstand to watch the races, you might as well stay at home, as from the other parts of the course it is difficult to see anything worthwhile.

This is as testing a course as the layout described above would suggest. In particular, the 5f and 6f races on the Hunt Cup course require considerable determination. **Penalised horses have a very poor record over this course and should never be backed.**

At sprint distances, this is very much a specialist's course and to be on the safe side your selection should have won over the course and distance. **Surprisingly, older horses often do well in 5f sprints**—if they have lost their edge at the starting gate they have time to recover (BRI EDEN and YOUNG INCA won races as 11 year olds here).

The Hunt Cup course gives horses with a strong late finish enough opportunities—as tired horses roll, plenty of gaps open up. It does not suit front runners, and I would be very cautious about backing a horse successful elsewhere with this style of running.

The course can get very waterlogged, and is subject to rapid changes of going particularly in the spring and autumn meetings. Make sure that you have up-to-the-minute information on the state of the going.

Sometimes the field divides into two unequal parts. If a horse races virtually alone but runs well or if on the unfavoured side, it should be noted for the future (for example, TREMBLANT 1985).

There is a good standard of racing at every meeting here, and in recent years there has been a notable improvement in the quality of the September meeting.

The Royal Ascot meeting in mid-June remains supreme in the handicap racing calendar. Interestingly, this is not the case for the two year old races which have declined steadily in the last 20 years.

It is hard to find winners at this meeting, although easy to eliminate losers. Horses which have won a plate at a weak meeting, and are then entered for these highly competitive handicaps stand virtually no chance. Likewise, winners from the Epsom Derby meeting—the courses are totally different. Sometimes you can turn this to your advantage, as such winners are often strongly supported in the market. If you have a strong selection in the same race, do not hesitate if your horse is pushed out in price: an Epsom winner really offers very little competition. This is one of the very few meetings where there is a reasonably strong betting market, so if you have a good fancy you will get a good price.

Essentially you should regard this as a very good meeting for observation— almost every year horses which win or run well can be placed to win shortly afterwards. However, these handicaps are very strongly contested, and it often takes the winner some time to recover from his exertions.

KEY RACES
Victoria Cup (April meeting, 7f. As this is run over a specialist distance, if a horse wins this in good style he has a good chance in the 7f **Bunbury Cup** at the Newmarket July meeting (MUMMY'S PLEASURE 1984; TREMBLANT 1985) . However, this is no longer the race it was, and it may not be such a useful pointer in the future. Like several of the other big handicaps earlier in the season, it is now somewhat overshadowed by the much more valuable 7f handicap run at the September meeting.

Royal Hunt Cup (Royal Ascot meeting, 8f): good winners of the **Whitsun Cup**, Sandown, do well here. But a previous winner must carry less than 8–7, and be in the top third of the drawn numbers (HAWKLEY 1984). Although it is a furlong less, a convincing winner of this race can go well in the 7f **Bunbury Cup** at the Newmarket July meeting (PATRIACH 1986).

Bessborough Stakes (Royal Ascot meeting, 12f): very difficult to find the winner. When the Newbury **Summer Cup** was a more competitive race, it was often a pointer to the race. However, the winner here can do well in the **Old Newton Cup** at Haydock (CLANTIME 1985; PIPSTED 1987).

King George V Stakes (Royal Ascot meeting, 12f 3 year olds): a good qualification is a convincing win in one of the 10f races at Newmarket (MOON MADNESS 1986).

Wokingham Stakes (Royal Ascot meeting 6f): this is one of the top sprint handicaps of the year. It is very difficult to find any pointers—but it is a great race for observations. Any horse which finishes well (and usually 2 lengths cover the first 9 home) can be found a sprint handicap soon afterwards (MANIM-STAR 1986).

Britannia Stakes (Royal Ascot meeting, 8f 3 year olds): this is the most difficult and the least informative of the Royal Ascot handicaps. The field is usually full of 'dark horses', which are difficult to win with if successful here, as the handicapper usually errs on the side of caution when attempting to assess the winner. Be wary of backing the winner of this race, however well he runs, if he comes out fairly quickly (say at the Newmarket July meeting: FOREIGN SURVIVOR 1988).

From about 1986 onwards, the handicaps at the Autumn meetings have received greatly increased prize money. It is too early to forecast the effect this will have on the structure of handicaps, but it is already clear that winners are hard to find at these meetings.

Ayr

LAYOUT: for races of 7f and over, a left-handed oval, with well graded turns to a 4f run in; slight undulations—galloping in character, a good test, and does not favour any type of horse.

The 6f course is straight and very wide, giving plenty of room in sprints.

GOING: on sandy soil, the course drains well, and rarely gets very heavy. However, when the going does get soft, the course does not drain evenly, and the ground near the stands rail is often faster than the rest of the course.

DRAW: high numbers usually have an advantage on the straight course, particularly when soft; in big fields over 7f and 8f a low draw is best.

The racing here is of good quality, and the form of high-class handicap races is worth following elsewhere. However, I do not generally bet here, except at the excellent 4 day Western Meeting in September. A word of caution—this meeting usually has soft to heavy going, so it is essential to check that your selection is suited to this type of ground.

Ayr Gold Cup (Western meeting, 6f): the winner of the **Portland Handicap,** Doncaster, is usually entered for this race, but only rarely succeeds in carrying the penalty (DAWN'S DELIGHT 1987). It is better to look among the close-up horses which have run well, although only if they have shown form on the going.

Bath

LAYOUT: 12f 25y left-handed oval, with a sharp bend to the 3f run in. This rises slightly, on a gradual curve.

The 5f 167 yards and 5f course join the main course on the run in.

GOING: a downland course, this usually provides good going. All the meetings last only one day, so the turf gets plenty of time to recover.

DRAW: in races up to 8f, advantage for low numbers.

Despite the bends, this is quite a galloping course, providing a good test. This is something of a specialist's course and winners here can win again.

Beverley

LAYOUT: 11f left-handed course, with a steep bend downhill into the 2½f run-in, uphill all the way.

The separate 5f course, uphill all the way, joins the main course with a distinct elbow.

GOING: during the summer months, usually firm; before the watering system was improved, it used to get rather hard.

DRAW: high numbers have an advantage on the 5f course.

Because of the downhill turn, the round course is sharp rather than galloping. **The 5f course is severe, and it is risky backing top weights and penalised horses. Form from the easier northern courses, such as Thirsk, does not work out here.**

Good class stakes horses sometimes run here (for example, in the **Hilary Needler Trophy,** for 2 year old fillies), but the handicappers are usually moderate.

Brighton

LAYOUT: The 12f course (the longest distance) is something of a switchback: uphill 3f; a slight descent and ascent; a sharp downhill for 3f; a rise to the winning post of 12′ at 1/55, then 100 yards flat.

GOING: the chalk soil drains well, and the going rarely gets really heavy.

DRAW: low numbers are favoured, particularly in sprints. A fast start is essential.

The course resembles Epsom, although the finish here is more severe than at Epsom and often finds out runners which seem to have set up an unassailable lead. Course winners, particularly over 12f, have a good record, as do top weights. If they can cope with the final hill, front runners do well here.

However, the standard of racing is generally moderate and it is difficult to find a good bet. Sometimes a good accelerating type (eg LADY GERARD 1983; GOUVERNO 1983; SWINGING REBEL 1984; GURTEEN BOY 1985; RASLAAN 1988) is on show here.

Carlisle

LAYOUT: a 13f right-handed pear-shaped course, 3f downhill at the start then mainly flat, turns quite sharply into the straight uphill run in of 3½f.

The 6f course (including the 5f) starts on a chute, bears right after 1½f and when it joins the main course.

GOING: can get very holding, as the subsoil is clay.

DRAW: high numbers may have an advantage up to 8f.

Quite a galloping track, the sprint course being particularly severe. Top weights are at a disadvantage here, especially when the going is soft.

Catterick

LAYOUT: 8f 180y left-handed oval, with a straight 3f run in. The 7f track joins the round course at the 6f marker, runs downhill to the run in. The 5f course is set on a 2f spur, runs sharply downhill at first, then with marked undulations.

GOING: as the subsoil is gravel, the going can change quite rapidly. Late in the season the turf often gets very cut up.

DRAW: at 5f, 6f and 7f, low numbers have an advantage.

The handy type is greatly favoured here, because of the surface undulations. Front runners do well here. Top weights are not necessarily at disadvantage, jockeyship and previous experience of the course count for more.

Chepstow

LAYOUT: a 16f left-handed oval, with a straight run of 5f which has very marked undulations.
The straight 8f course runs downhill to the round course.
GOING: tends to be rather hard in a hot summer.
DRAW: nothing in it.
This is a difficult course to figure out—the undulations in the straight prevent horses from going a good gallop, but do not seem to favour top weights or any particular kind of horse.
Flat racing here is distinctly moderate—the National Hunt meetings are far superior.

Chester

LAYOUT: a 8f 73y left-handed circle, quite flat, with a straight 2f run in.
GOING: nothing significant.
DRAW: up to 7f 122y a low draw is regarded as essential.
Chester is more like a greyhound track or an American course, with its tight bends and clear visibility from the stand. The May meeting attracts good class pattern racers, but the handicaps are not quite of this quality.
The big, galloping type of horse usually fails to act here; top weights of the right conformation certainly have a good chance. Sprinters must make a quick start, as there is virtually no chance of catching up. **This is very much a course for 'hard luck' stories, and I regard Chester form as completely unreliable.**

Doncaster

LAYOUT: the left-handed round course is 15f and quite flat, except for a hillock at the 8f mark, with sweeping turns leading to a 4½f run in. There is an 8f course which starts from a chute on one of the turns. The straight 8f course is very wide and gives plenty of room for a late challenge.
GOING: the springy turf provides one the best racing surfaces in England. It drains well and does not get too hard.
DRAW: unless the going is soft, the high numbers in the draw have a definite advantage in big fields on the straight course, but on the round mile a low draw is a big advantage especially in large fields.
This is a galloping course, ideal for the strongly built long-striding stayer.
Doncaster is rather out of fashion as a course at the moment, despite its excellent physical characteristics. The first big handicap of the season, the **Lincoln,** is one of our handicaps to avoid—there is no current form, and a great deal depends on the draw.
I rarely find an opportunity here, except at the St. Leger meeting in September where there are a number of high-class, well-contested handicaps, usually run on good to firm going.
Portland Handicap (St. Leger meeting, 5f 140 yards): form works out well in this race, and winners last time out have a good record. Winners of this event are often entered for the **Ayr Gold Cup,** but rarely carry a penalty with success.

Edinburgh

LAYOUT: just under 10f right-handed oval, with sharp bends leading to a 4f run in, virtually flat.

The 5f course is set on an extension, at a slight angle.

GOING: laid out on sand, drains well and gives consistently good going.

DRAW: seems to have little effect.

The course favours the well-balanced type, and top weights have a good chance here, as they cannot really go an all-out gallop.

Epsom

LAYOUT: a left-handed 'U' shaped course, the 12f is uphill for the first 4f, level for about 2f, then downhill round Tattenham corner to the 4f run in to the finish, downhill to the final furlong, followed by a rise to the winning post.

The 5f course is straight and joins the main course at Tattenham Corner. It has a fall of 32' at 1/23 followed by a fall of 40' at 1/57. The 6f 9y and 7f 11y course join the main course at a tangent. The course also slopes across from the stands rails to the other side of the track.

GOING: rarely becomes hard, but can become very soft at the Spring meeting. Because of the camber the going can vary from good to soft on the same day, which can give misleading results.

DRAW: a low draw is an advantage at 6f and 7f but nowadays a high draw is considered best at 5f.

Only the Epsom Derby meeting attracts good quality handicappers, and then (I suspect) so that their owners can have a runner on Derby or Oaks day. The other meetings (in April and at the end of August) are generally of mediocre quality, as often are some of the handicap races at the Derby meeting itself. Exceptionally, winners of 0–75 handicaps at lower class courses can win here.

Epsom has declined as a training centre during the last decade, as several of the stables and gallops have been sold to builders. Many of the top flight trainers from other areas, in particular Newmarket, seem unwilling to enter their horses for these handicaps, despite the more than adequate prize money. **Local trainers are always worth considering here, as their animals train on the Downs.**

The course favours the handy well-balanced type of horse; long-striding gallopers sometimes lose their action completely when coming round Tattenham corner. Watch the races closely at this point to see if it is failure to act on the course which has ruined their chances—up to this point, it is quite a galloping course.

Course winners and top weights must always be considered here. A fast start is essential for runners in the 5f sprint—the fastest 5f course in the world.

Epsom is not an easy course to ride—apprentices in particular often find it difficult to stop their horses from hanging towards the far rails and thus causing interference.

Folkestone

LAYOUT: an 11f right-handed pear-shaped course, with gentle turns leading to a straight run in of 2½f. This course has minor undulations and a gentle rise in the last furlong. The straight 6f course also undulates for its first 3½ furlongs till joining the round course.

GOING: in wet weather, can get very holding quite quickly.

DRAW: no noticeable advantage.

This is not a galloping track, and top weights have quite a good record. The 12f 0–75 handicaps do not take a great deal of winning, and previous winners can often win with a penalty. Course winners should always be carefully scrutinised. Because of the undemanding nature of the course, Folkestone form cannot be taken with confidence to other tracks.

Goodwood

LAYOUT: the 12f course runs away uphill, then follows a series of undulations till it joins the straight course by quite a tight right-handed bend.

The straight 6f course has a steep rise of 12' at 1/55 in the first furlong, then falls 14' in the next two hundred yards, then flattens to become level near the winning post.

GOING: beautifully laid turf on a chalk subsoil, usually drains well and does not get too firm. However, when the going gets soft, the course does drain unevenly.

DRAW: high numbers have a definite advantage in big fields on the straight course.

The course is in a beautiful setting on the Sussex Downs; but always be prepared for the worst meteorologically. When the squalls come in from the English Channel, you can get drenched through very quickly.

The course does live up to its name of 'Glorious' for the July meeting but at the other meetings although the prize money is reasonable the handicaps are often quite moderate.

The steep hill at the beginning of the 6f course allows slow starters a chance, but, as at Epsom, there is little chance of regaining ground lost at the start of the 5f course.

At the other distances the course is much better suited to the handy type than to the big long-striding galloper. Because of the curves and the gradients, the field rarely goes full tilt until it gets to the run-in, so top weights are in with a chance here. The bend into the sprint course is quite sharp, and horses sometimes lose their chance by running wide here. If the going is soft, accidents sometimes happen at this point.

I find Goodwood form something of a puzzle. The July meeting form usually provides pointers to later winners, but it often completely fails to work out at more testing courses, such as Newbury or Newmarket. The Lingfield meeting immediately before the July meeting sometimes provides a pointer (DIABOLI-CAL LIBERTY 1983; ARADU 1988), but as a rule you should only consider form from the higher class courses.

Stewards Cup (July meeting, 6f): this race frequently provides a major upset (MADRACO 1987) and as a rule is to be avoided. Horses which do not win but are noted as running well can usually be placed to advantage elsewhere (GLENCROFT 1988).

Extel Handicap (July meeting, 10f 3 year olds): the top race of the season over this distance for 3 year olds. This is often won by a 'dark horse'—against the usual pattern, it may be won by a winner of a plate last time out (BROKEN HEARTED 1988). Quite often this race sets a real puzzle beforehand, and then is won with consummate ease. Winners usually graduate to non-handicap races on their next outing.

Hamilton

LAYOUT: the straight 6f course is extended to 13f by a right-handed loop with easy turns, completed 5½f out. The loop has a steady uphill rise, the straight is undulating, with a dip about 3f from the winning post. The layout has some resemblance to Salisbury.

GOING: given its clay subsoil, in wet weather, the dip can become rather testing.

DRAW: favours low numbers over 7f and 8f; in the soft, high numbers may have an advantage in 5f and 6f races.

The 6f course is quite a severe test, especially in soft going. The loop course is also fairly demanding, and peculiar enough to encourage course specialists. The general level of handicap racing cannot be said to be very high (the writer aims to be diplomatic), but a good winner of a reasonable race is worth following in similar class. Course specialists do well here.

Haydock Park

LAYOUT: a 13f round oval shaped course, with a sharp left hand bend into a straight 4f run-in, with a slight but steady rise throughout.

6f races start on a chute onto the round course; the 5f course is straight.

GOING: sometimes gets very heavy, particularly on the bends—when this happens you should definitely not bet. In heavy going, the pace is usually funereal and the results wildly unreliable.

DRAW: tends to favour low numbers over 6f, 7f and 8f; 5f races on soft ground, high numbers best.

The straight course provides reliable form, but races at distances of 7f 40 yards and over often give unreliable results. The problem seems to be the sharp bend into the straight—some horses do not handle this well, and there is often scrimmaging at this point.

The Old Newton Cup (12f July) should always be considered carefully if there is a winner over the distance from the Royal Ascot meeting.

Kempton Park

LAYOUT: the round course is flat, roughly triangular in shape, with sharp bends into a 3½f run in. The 10f Jubilee course is downhill at the start, curves gradually to the left and then runs straight for about 3f to join the round course.

Races up to 6f are run on a separate straight, flat course.

GOING: both courses drain well, because of the gravel subsoil.

DRAW: reckoned to be of little importance.

I consider that the round course gives top weights a chance, as the tight bends prevent the runners from going flat out; the Jubilee course is quite different, as they usually go a good gallop from the start, and it is a fair test of all types.

The Easter meeting usually has some good-class handicappers, and providing the going is not too soft, there are usually some flyers for the notebook. Occasionally if there is a good winner at Newmarket from the backend of the previous season running in the 10f Rosebery Handicap, it is worth backing (BAHOOR 1984; SLANGHI VAH 1987).

The early season meetings often feature good, improving horses (PERION 1986; STATEN ISLAND 1988), which can be followed at most other courses, except those with a stiff uphill finish, such as Newmarket or Sandown. Later in

51

the season (after Royal Ascot), the meetings are of a lower standard and although there are some high-grade handicaps, they rarely seem to attract good horses.

Lingfield Park

LAYOUT: the 10f round course is a left-handed loop, flat for the first 4f, rising sharply to a small hill, from which there is a steep 150 yards downhill turn into the straight. The remaining 3½ furlongs is less steeply downhill, with rising ground near the winning post.

The 7f 140y straight course (races are also run over this distance on the round course) is downhill to the junction with the round course.

GOING: despite recent improvements in drainage, the course can still become heavy quite quickly, especially in the spring and autumn.

DRAW: on the straight course low numbers may have the advantage when the going is heavy.

Lingfield is quite similar to Epsom—in fact, the downhill turn into the straight is probably steeper and sharper than Tattenham Corner. Both courses here are fast and not too testing, giving top weights a good chance. The standard of racing here is rather variable, perhaps on a par with Brighton, which it also resembles topographically. Winners over the 7f course have a good chance of winning here again (GOLD MINORIES 1988).

Leicester

LAYOUT: a 14f right-handed oval, with a run-in of 4½f.

The straight 8f course is downhill for about 4 furlongs, then has a sharp rise of 26 feet at 1/84 before levelling out to the winning post.

GOING: although the track drains quite well, at both ends of the season, the going can get quite heavy.

DRAW: no significant advantage.

The stiff uphill finish makes this quite a testing course, especially as the runners are able to go a good gallop in the earlier stages. Consequently Leicester form is very reliable and a useful pointer. Top weights are at a considerable disadvantage. Even when upgraded to Newmarket, horses which have run well here can follow up in a weak race (YOUNG JASON 1985; HOME BLADE 1985). 12f winners last time out at other stiff courses can go in here again.

Two words of warning, though: when the going gets soft, as it often does at the backend, upsets are frequent. At the end of the season Leicester seems a favourite venue for trainers with the handicappers which they haven't managed to place yet, resulting in very large fields and shock results.

Newbury

LAYOUT: 15f left-handed oval, with a 5f run in. There are 7f and 8f courses set off the round course.

The straight 8f course has slight undulations throughout.

GOING: can get quite heavy at the Spring meeting, but otherwise nothing to note.

DRAW: nothing significant.

On paper, the quality of handicap racing is high, with several races with good prizes—the Spring Cup, Summer Cup, Autumn Cup—spaced throughout the season. The standard of racing seems much higher before the Royal Ascot meeting. Thereafter, although the stakes races are hotly competed for, the handicaps are often somewhat lack lustre.

The races seem competitive, with the runners going a good gallop and a long run to the winning post. However, Newbury form should not be taken to courses with an uphill finish.

KEY RACES

Spring Cup (April 8f): not a very competitive handicap these days, as it comes rather early in the season. I cannot recommend any pointers to this race, nor can the result be followed with any confidence.

Summer Cup (June 12f): if there is a competitive field, a good winner or placed horse can win a 12f race at Royal Ascot after running well here.

Autumn Cup (September 13f 60 yds): although this is outside my usual distance range, a horse which has shown good form in the 14f 127yds handicap at the Doncaster St. Leger meeting often makes a good show here (EASTERN MYSTIC 1985).

The Highclere Nursery (September 7f): despite what I have said above, a good winner of this race can win a Newmarket nursery (CYRANO DE BERGERAC 1985; PRINT 1986).

Newcastle

LAYOUT: a 14f round course, with a 4f run in.

The straight course, for all races of 7f or less, has a gradual rise to the winning post: 6 feet at 1/122, 5 feet at 1/83 and 1 foot at 1/195.

GOING: the course now drains better than it used to, but can still get quite heavy at any time of the season.

DRAW: no significance.

Newcastle is an excellent course, and it is a pity that with the increasing concentration on southern racing it does not have enough racing to match. It is a fair and very testing track of a galloping character, and form can be relied on anywhere else.

The **Gosforth Park Cup** (5f June) and the **Northumberland Sprint Trophy** (6f July) often go to the winners of handicaps last time out.

Newmarket: July Course

LAYOUT: 2m long with a right handed bend after a mile. In the mile straight, it undulates for the first 6f, then falls 8 feet at 1/115, followed by a rise of 18 feet at 1/46, the steepest finish of any 'Flat' course.

Newmarket: Rowley Mile Course

LAYOUT: the 2m 2f Cesarewitch course begins on the July course, turns into the straight Rowley Mile with over 10f to go. It then undulates for the first 10f, runs downhill at 1/90 for a furlong into the Dip, then rises 11 feet at 1/65 in the final furlong to the winning post.

GOING: on both courses, the best in the country. It seldom becomes hard even in the hottest summer; and drains very well and quickly throughout the season so that it is rarely heavier than soft. Horses which have shown a preference for soft going at other courses find that good going here suitable to their running style.

DRAW: no significance.

Newmarket fully deserves its title of 'Headquarters'. It is, as an Edwardian writer put it, '21 lbs and a beating' in front of any other racecourse. The racing is almost invariably of good class, and even the 2 (0–75) handicaps are quite well-contested. Only the second July Meeting and the August meetings are somewhat below the general standard of the Newmarket season.

The wide, galloping courses with their relentless uphill finishes test a horse to his limits. There can be no hard luck stories here—and a horse which wins well at Newmarket with a strong late finish can be followed with complete confidence anywhere else. Here, too, you don't have to worry about large fields—as tired horses roll on the uphill finishes, plenty of gaps open up.

Horses often bunch together in the middle stages of a race, allowing late finishers to be covered up. **It takes quite an unusual horse and a super-confident jockey to make all the running here and win.**

The sprint races, which are almost all over 6f, are usually won by the horses which make their challenge at some point in the final furlong. Newmarket provides some of the closest finishes of any course—not only is this exciting, it is good news for the private handicapper.

Consequently I rate Newmarket form highest of all; and good form also works out very well here.

I don't think that Newmarket favours course specialists in the way that, say, Brighton or Epsom does, but I certainly regard a previous course and distance win as a great advantage.

Because the going has relatively few variations, time figures from Newmarket are very reliable, and a winner which records a good time here in a sprint handicap is worth following.

Two words of warning. Top weights have to be really big strong types to carry the weight; and apprentices often find the big open spaces too much of a problem and cannot prevent their horses wandering all over the place.

KEY RACES

The early season **10f Across the Flat** Races are a tremendous test (SEA CHIMES 1979; MOON MADNESS 1986; MERCE CUNNINGHAM 1988); and good winners at Newmarket can be relied on to do well at Royal Ascot. Late improving two year olds run well in the end of season nurseries.

Bunbury Cup (7f July): not quite the competitive handicap it used to be, but look for a distance winner (1985 TREMBLANT). At the other July meeting handicaps, late-finishing winners from Sandown have a good record (COURTING SEASON 1984; AVENTINO 1986; HELLO VAIGLY 1988).

Two handicaps to avoid are the **Cambridgeshire** (9f) and the **Cesarewitch** (2m 2f), which invariably produce shock results.

Nottingham

LAYOUT: 12f left-handed oval, with easy turns into a final run in of approximately 2½ furlongs; flat throughout.

The straight, flat 6f course joins the round course after just over 1f.

GOING: nothing to note.

DRAW: does not seem to give any advantage.

Nottingham seems rather a 'neutral' track, not favouring any particular kind of horse. Improving handicappers rarely seem to emerge from its rather uninspiring programme. The 6f **Stewards' Cup** (August) is not the race it was, although always worth considering if there is a runner from the Goodwood July meeting.

Pontefract

LAYOUT: a 16f left-handed oval, with a straight run-in of only just over 2f. The bends are sharp; and there are two rises and two falls until the final steep rise over the last 3f.

GOING: can get rather hard during a hot summer.

DRAW: in sprints, a low draw is a great advantage.

The final climb is very punishing, especially in the soft. Despite this, because of the earlier turns and changes of level, it is not a galloping course. Top weights cannot be said to have an advantage; nor does the course seem to favour any type of horse. In fact, Pontefract is rather a puzzle: previous experience of the course is the safest guide, and there have been several course specialists. A fast start is essential in sprints.

Redcar

LAYOUT: a left-handed oval, with rather tight bends leading to a 5f run-in, flat throughout. The 8f course is set on a straight, flat extension.

GOING: nothing significant.

DRAW: no advantages.

Redcar has rather suffered from being in the wrong half of the Two Nations. From the early 1960s to the mid-seventies, it was a very popular course, with good quality handicaps, such as the **Zetland Gold Cup** (10f May), which were well-contested. In the last decade or so, the quality of racing here has noticeably declined—a pity, because this is a good galloping course which is a fair test of all types of horses. However, in the last three years, there have been signs of a revival with good horses winning the **Zetland Gold Cup** (FRIDU 1988; INAAD 1989).

Top weights have no advantages.

Ripon

LAYOUT: a right-handed 13f oval, with rather tight bends leading to a wide 5f run-in, which has a slight dip at the distance. The 6f course is set on a straight extension.

GOING: good turf; the clay subsoil over gravel seems to drain well.

DRAW: no advantages.

The course does not favour any kind of runner or top weight. In August it stages one of the best sprint handicaps in the north, the **Great St. Wilfrid** (6f). This is always worth considering, and often goes to a winner last time out or a horse with good recent form.

Salisbury

LAYOUT: a right-handed loop with a run in of 7f. The 8f course is set on a spur, which joins the loop course for the last 7 furlongs. However, this is not straight, but has an elbow at the 5f marker followed by a steady ascent throughout the last 4f. It is rather like Hamilton in layout.

GOING: a downland course based on chalk, good conditions in dry weather, but can be very holding when it gets wet.

DRAW: a low draw is a definite advantage when the ground rides soft.

The uphill finish makes this a severe testing course—Salisbury form is very reliable as a result, and some high-class handicappers have first shown their mettle here (TREMBLANT 1984). Sprint winners here in good style always worth noting, especially if they have recorded a good time (SILENT MAJORITY 1986). Winners here can do well at Newmarket or Sandown, and vice versa (DISMISS 1988).

The racing is of rather uneven quality here—the Bibury Cup meeting (June) has fallen away rather sadly in recent years, but the early season meetings often attract good quality handicappers. An excellent course, strongly recommended for a good day out. The best vantage point is high up in the stand in the Tattersalls enclosure.

Sandown

LAYOUT: a 13f oval course, level until the 4f run in, of which all bar the last level hundred yards is uphill. The bend into the straight is rather tight.

The separate straight 5f course rises steadily uphill throughout.

GOING: never gets too hard.

DRAW: on the 5f course, high numbers have a big advantage when the going is soft.

Sandown is a great place to go racing: it is easy to watch even the distance racing for the whole circuit you can get high up above the course to see the finish; and the stand, paddock and winner's enclosure are very compactly laid out. The only drawbacks are that the 5f course is some way from the stands, with the winning post set at an angle to the stands; and, likewise, the main course does not run parallel to the grandstand.

Sandown attracts good class stakes horses with its 6 pattern races, but the standard of handicap races is, in my opinion, rather variable. There does not seem to be any pattern throughout the season, except for the Hong Kong meeting early in July at which the standard is generally high. Otherwise, some of the other meetings at any time of the season have races which are best described as 'weakly contested'.

Although the runners go a good gallop on the back straight, they do slow down considerably to negotiate the turn. In my view, this gives the top weights a chance and they have quite a good record here. Front runners can also do well, and sometimes 'steal' a race, showing form not confirmed by subsequent performance (eg MY BUDDY 1987). To win here, a horse must show that he can act on an uphill finish.

The 5f course is a different matter altogether. There is no other 5f course quite like it. Sometimes 6f horses are put back to 5f here, in the view that their stamina will tell, but it seems to be a different kind of test. I find that to be on the safe side you should only back a previous course/distance winner here (eg SILENT MAJORITY 1986); and I would not recommend backing penalised winners here. But good winners can be relied on at other courses with an uphill finish (UMBELATA 1987; JOYTOTHEWORLD 1988).

KEY RACES

Esher Cup (8f three-year-olds April): usually won by an improving horse (RAYKOUR 1988; TOP-BOOT 1989).

Whitsun Cup (8f May): a winner of this race in good style can win another good class handicap (HAWKLEY 1984; WAAJIB 1987; INAAD 1988).

GRE handicap (8f Hong Kong meeting July): sometimes a pointer to the 8f handicap at the Newmarket July meeting (COURTING SEASON 1984; AVENTINO 1986).

Thirsk

LAYOUT: a 10f left-handed oval, with easy bends leading to a 4f slightly undulating run-in. The 6f course is set on a straight extension on which the undulations are more pronounced.

GOING: nothing to note.

DRAW: high numbers have something of an advantage on the straight course.

A perfectly fair course, offering no advantages to any particular kind of horse. Before the Royal Ascot meeting, it sometimes attracts early season winners from better class courses; but on the other hand it is rare that a Thirsk winner goes on to anything better once the high season has started.

Warwick

LAYOUT: a 14f nearly circular left-handed course, with tight bends leading to a wide run-in of about 3½f.

The 5f runs straight for 1½f then has a left-hand elbow to the main course.

GOING: with a clay subsoil, it can get very holding in the spring and autumn.

DRAW: up to 8f high numbers have an advantage when the going is soft.

What it lacks in quality, Warwick makes up in its quantity of (0–75) handicaps. The October meeting often attracts large fields, especially for the nurseries—if run on soft going, they are the nearest thing to equine bingo I know.

For different reasons, this course is as much a puzzle as Pontefract. There is usually a good gallop in the back straight, but the runners are slowed down by the bend into the straight. Thus the galloping types are at an advantage in the early part of the races of 7f and over, until the bend puts paid to their chances. It might be expected that the top weights would have a good chance here, but it doesn't seem to work out like that.

Windsor

LAYOUT: a figure of 8 with a nearly straight 5f run in; flat throughout.

GOING: usually good.

DRAW: in the 5f and 6f races, high numbers seem to have an advantage, if they can get away quickly enough.

There is plenty of racing here, with evening meetings almost every week from the beginning of May to the end of August. The handicaps are usually of rather average quality, although the early season handicaps (up to the time of the Royal Ascot meeting) are markedly better than those run later on in the season.

Most handicaps here involve tried and tested performers which have raced against each other on this course several times. In this respect, racing here is much more like American racing or greyhound racing than at any other British course. It's difficult to find a good bet here, which is unfortunate given that the betting market is relatively strong, because of the large crowds of London punters.

Surprisingly the 10f plates which carry rather minimal prize money attract horses which later turn out distinctly useful (BEDTIME 1983; MILLFONTAINE 1983).

Its unique configuration for a Flat racecourse (though Fontwell Park, the National Hunt course, is very similar) encourages course specialists. Top weights have a chance here, as often the early stages of the races are run at no great pace.

Wolverhampton

LAYOUT: a 12f left-handed triangular course, flat, with quite well-graduated turns into a straight 4f run in.

The 5f 190y course is set on a flat, straight extension.

GOING: rarely gets hard in the summer, nor does it get too heavy.

DRAW: no advantage.

This is quite a galloping course, and top weights have no advantage here. The rather grandly named **Midland Cambridgeshire** (9f 0–100 August) and the **Midland Cesarewitch** (2m 1f 0–100 September) are well above the standard of the other handicaps here.

Oddly enough for a course which seems to have no particular characteristics, the sprint course seems to attract specialists, such as BRI-EDEN and RELATIVE EASE in the late 1970s.

Yarmouth

LAYOUT: a 13f left-handed oval, flat throughout, with tight turns, leading to a 5f run-in.

The 8f course is set on a straight flat extension.

GOING: nothing to note.

DRAW: high numbers may have an advantage on the straight course.

Although the turns are tight, the long straight run-in discounts any advantages which might be gained by top weights. Newmarket trainers often use this track as a trial ground, which raises the class of some races above what is justified by their prize money. However, be warned that form from Yarmouth is generally unreliable.

York

LAYOUT: a 16f left-handed U shaped course, wide and flat throughout, with a wide sweeping turn to a 5f run in.

7f races have a straight 2f spur onto the round course; straight 6f and 5f course.

GOING: the course does not drain well, and the going can change to soft very quickly. Since the course does not drain evenly, soft going usually produces shock results. Therefore up-to-the-minute information is essential, and unless the going is good and the sun is shining, do not bet here.

DRAW: low numbers favoured over 5f and 6f when the going is soft.

York is a splendid place for watching the races, especially if you can get onto the flat-roofed stand about 100 yards before the finish. In my opinion this is the best view in the whole of British racing.

The track is ideal for the long-striding galloper, and there is little excuse for hard luck stories here. Top weights have to be really well built to win at this course.

The May meeting attracts good class handicappers but is a little early in the season. I find the later meetings better for finding winners, but even during the summer and early autumn, be on your guard as the going can get soft in a matter of hours. To repeat my warning above, you really need to know the state of the going at the moment of the off, not just on the morning of the race. To be on the safe side, avoid betting at York unless the going is good and the sun is shining.

I have classified together courses by groups. The following courses do not appear in this list because I find them very difficult to classify—the reader is referred to the description above: Catterick Chepstow Chester Nottingham Thirsk Warwick Yarmouth.

COURSES WITH AN UPHILL FINISH
Ascot Bath Beverley Carlisle Hamilton Haydock Leicester Newcastle Newmarket (July and Rowley Mile courses) Salisbury Sandown (sprints and distance courses)

FLAT, GALLOPING COURSES
Ayr Doncaster Kempton (all courses) Newbury Redcar Ripon Wolverhampton York

UNDULATING COURSES FAVOURING FRONT RUNNERS
Brighton Epsom Lingfield

COURSES FAVOURING TOP WEIGHTS
Brighton Edinburgh Epsom Folkestone Goodwood Kempton (round course) Lingfield Sandown

COURSES FAVOURING SPECIALISTS
Ascot Brighton Folkestone Hamilton Pontefract Sandown (5f)Windsor Wolverhampton (sprints)

THE MOST RELIABLE FORM COURSES (in alphabetical order)
Ascot Hamilton Leicester Newcastle Newmarket (July and Rowley Mile courses) Salisbury Sandown (sprints and distance courses)

RACING IN IRELAND

As in France, racing in Ireland is centralised around the capital city. The form from the courses on the Dublin 'circuit'—Leopardstown, Phoenix Park, and The Curragh—is of much higher value than that from the provinces. It is most unwise to bet on form taken from the provincial courses.

Irish handicap racing differs in two significant respects from its British counterpart—one of which is an advantage, the other a disadvantage, for the backer.

Ireland has maintained the entry system which operated in Britain until the end of the 1988 season, before the introduction of the present 5 day entry system. Entries are usually made about 3 weeks before the date of the race, and the handicap marks are set at that point. Therefore, the period during which penalties can be incurred is much longer than in Britain—thus the advantage which the backer can gain from backing a penalised horse is enhanced. In my view, this more than outweighs the disadvantage. Races aren't graded (this change was introduced in Britain in the early 1970s), so you have to judge by the level of the prize money and the general standard of a race. However, as in Britain, the only sure guide to the competitiveness of a race is the mark allocated to the top weight. Unfortunately, the handicap marks are not published in the press at all—you have to subscribe to *The Irish Racing Calendar* (obtainable from: The Turf Club, The Curragh, County Kildare, Ireland) in order to find out what they are.

LEOPARDSTOWN
LAYOUT: a left-handed oval track 14 furlongs round, with a 2½ furlong uphill run in. It has a straight 6 furlongs course.

GOING: nothing significant.

DRAW: on the 6f course, low numbers are at a disadvantage.

Its layout was inspired by that of Sandown Park, to which it bears some resemblance. Although the run in is about 1½ furlongs shorter than at Sandown, this is a testing finish which gives reliable results.

PHOENIX PARK
LAYOUT: a flat, easy track. Races from 5f up to 10f are run right-handed round the course; those over 11f are run left; and there is a straight 5f.

GOING: as at other Irish courses, heavy rain and a change of going within a fairly short space of time, is always a possibility to take into consideration.

DRAW: in sprints, high numbers are favoured when the stalls are on the stands' side; and vice versa.

THE CURRAGH
LAYOUT: a round course of 16 furlongs, with easy turns leading to a straight run in of 3 furlongs and an uphill finish. Races up to 6 furlongs 63 yards are straight, with a chute off the course, allowing for 7 furlongs and 8 furlongs races.

GOING: usually quite good.

DRAW: on the straight course, law numbers are favoured when the stalls are on the stands side.

In all, the straight mile rises by 29 feet, making this the greatest rise on any British or Irish course. This is a thorough test of stamina, and the combination of an uphill finish and a wide course gives every opportunity to the strong late finisher. Consequently form from The Curragh is of the highest value; and to bet here, you should only consider form from this course.

CHAPTER SEVEN
Jockeys and Trainers

It always surprises me how much the racing press concentrates on the human factor in the racing scene. Comment on how races are run or the condition of the runners is far outweighed by fascinating 'human interest' stories, such as why the horse was named after the owner's wife's dog or whatever.

However, the human factor cannot be completely ignored. In order of importance I put trainers a short head in front of jockeys in their contribution to winning races.

Trainers

In the last decade, several excellent publications like *Trainers Record* have come to the fore which analyse the records of trainers—preferred courses, type of horse, first time out winners, time of season and so on.

This has become something of a fashion, which may go the way of other fashions. For example, you only have to go back a few years to recall the time when reports of training gallops were all the rage. The press carried glowing reports of horses which could catch pigeons on the home gallops—and then on the course they couldn't catch a lame tortoise.

It always amazed me how much notice punters took of reports such as: 'of this group of horses so-and-so went best of all on the gallops'. You don't know how they were ridden and how much weight they are carrying. Look through the sporting press today—how often do you see such reports prominently featured?

While it is true that most trainers do work to a recognisable pattern, it would be quite illogical to base your selections on this. The two creatures which tend to be forgotten in the kind of second-guessing game—'Trainer X wouldn't be sending that horse all the way to racecourse Y if he didn't think he had a chance'—are the horse and the owner. You really are guessing about the horse's ability.

Trainers have improved their status from the pre-war days when Lord Derby treated them as glorified stable lads—but the owner still pays the bills and calls the tune. A horse *may* be sent a long way, say to Ayr from Newmarket, because the owner wishes to see his horse run at Ayr to impress a business colleague or friend, or for some other reason not strictly connected with the horse's form.

In any case, these patterns can change quite quickly. For instance, for several years, Geoff Lewis had a very good record at the Epsom Derby meeting. In recent years, he has not and has moved his operation elsewhere because he has a different type of horse.

Even if you do see that a trainer is following his pattern by sending horses to a minor meeting, eg Luca Cumani at Carlisle, you won't be the only person to notice such an obvious fact—even if you have found a winner, it will not be at a very attractive price.

Finally, there is one simple but crushing objection to making a system out of the analysis of trainers' record alone. Which horse do you choose when *two or more* trainers have followed their pattern by entering horses for a particular race?

This is not to say that there is no point in studying the abilities of the various

trainers. What we are looking for is the ability to keep improving horses 'on the boil' and place them to best advantage. But to know which trainers can do this it is not sufficient to look at the list of top trainers, or to look only at one year's record of trainers.

Most, but not all of the trainers who regularly appear in the top twenty for numbers of winners trained can be relied on to do this with handicappers. But note that I say 'most, but not all'. The reader should make his own analysis, but the handicap record of at least two of these trainers is not on a par with their training of Group horses.

In one case, they are too highly tried after an encouraging win which shows that they have improved considerably; in the other, they often disappoint after a good win. In neither case, is it a matter of incompetence—just that they have large strings, in which the Group/Classic horses must have the priority.

Apart from these, there are one or two leading trainers who do not quite get the best out of their handicappers. Perhaps this is carping, but I get the impression that some horses they place to win two quick races in succession, with nothing to follow, could have been placed to better advantage. I am not talking through my pocket—it was equally clear after their first win that they had a considerable amount in hand as it was after their second that they would now be pegged back by the handicapper.

What we must learn to recognise is the trainer who given the right material knows how to place in the handicap system. It is perhaps invidious to give examples, but two come to mind almost immediately—L G Cottrell and R V Smyth.

L G Cottrell is a very astute trainer of sprint handicappers (YOUNG INCA, EVER SHARP, GALLANT HOPE). In fact, one often finds that sprint handicappers which set up a sequence are trained by the smaller stables. Perhaps the bigger yards find them too much trouble—after all they run far more often during the season, and do not figure in the breeding world, several of the best of this type being geldings.

As an example of a well planned campaign, R V Smyth's handling of TREMBLANT could not be bettered. He won two handicaps in his third year, at Salisbury and Newmarket; and in his fourth year (1985) was placed to win the Victoria Cup (Ascot), the Bunbury Cup (Newmarket), a (0–100) at the St. Leger meeting—all over 7f, finishing off the season by winning the 9f Cambridgeshire.

Always be alert to the influence of a change of stables. A horse which does not run well for one perfectly capable trainer may run much better when transferred to another no more capable handler. Sometimes horses, like human beings, get stale and need a change of scene or routine. Stuck in a rut, a sprint handicapper may get down to a very attractive mark, and his new stable may be able to reap the benefits.

Equally, some trainers have the ability to 'repair' horses which have broken down in training. The transformation effected by David Chapman on CHAPLIN'S CLUB in 1985 was quite astounding, and there are some (but not many) other trainers who can bring new life to formerly moderate handicappers.

If you have a well-handicapped horse prepared by a competent trainer, how much influence is exercised by the other human factor, the jockey?

Jockeys

Of the present jockeys, I doubt if any of those who take it in turn to be champion have much more than 3lbs in hand of the good average types. I would never allow the fact that one of the champions is due to ride one of the top-rated override any of the other factors.

While Lester Piggott was riding, I would make his mount my selection even when it was two or three pounds out on the handicap. I am afraid that at the moment there is no one of the calibre of Lester Piggott—given that he was one of the three or four greatest jockeys ever to ride in Britain, that's not surprising. In my opinion he retired about 5 years too early.

His greatest strength was his versatility—he would ride different kinds of races on different kinds of horses. **Lester could ride *every* kind of race—making all, driving a horse out, coming with a late flourish, or waiting in front (even in a sprint, the most difficult of all).**

But above all it was Lester's ability to win a handicap by the narrowest possible margin with something in hand which must have been the official handicapper's nightmare—no jockey currently riding can do this so consistently.

It's quite possible to be champion jockey in some seasons and know how to ride only one kind of race—notably, a rider who is good at a driving finish can win enough races that way to be champion. **Some jockeys who for various accidental reasons do not command the best rides are in fact more talented—Tony Ives and John Reid spring to mind.**

Instead of blindly following a jockey's fortunes, learn to watch how jockeys ride. It used to be said of Sir Gordon Richards that the time to get anxious if you had backed one of his rides was when he sat still—he was trying to nurse his mount home. In particular, learn to detect what jockeys will do at the 2 furlong marker—with some jockeys even one or two efforts at rousting the horse along are a bad sign, as it means there is little left in reserve. When others begin to drive along vigorously at this point, there is not necessarily anything to worry about.

Apprentices

How do you weigh up (literally) the significance of the apprentice's allowance? At present, in Flat racing, they receive 7 lbs until they have won 10 races; 5 lbs until 50 winners; and 3 lbs until 75 winners.

There are no set rules, but some fairly clear guidelines. The average 7lbs claimer never gets beyond this stage, and his inexperience or lack of ability offsets any weight advantage from the claim. But if you follow racing closely, you will soon realise that there even some 7lbs claimers who ride as well as the average jockey. One well-known professional backer made large sums in the early '50s by selectively backing Lester Piggott's mounts—with the advantage of hindsight, a mouth-watering idea.

A good apprentice, therefore, is worth his weight in gold, and you should look for the occasions when his pull in the weights can be made to pay. For example, if he rides a penalised winner, where last time out a regular jockey was engaged, the apprentice allowance effectively discounts the penalty.

Less obviously, in some handicaps winners of apprentice races are not penalised and next time out can be ridden again by the apprentice—a kind of double bonus. Some trainers (in recent years Henry Candy) are particularly astute at this.

Finally, it is always worth looking at an apprentice's 'outside' rides, ie for a stable for which he does not normally ride. Every winning ride brings nearer the fateful day when he can no longer claim, and a good trainer will try to ensure that he makes the maximum use of his allowance.

In all these cases, it is not enough to note with enthusiasm that your selection has a good claiming apprentice. You must ask two further questions.

Can he ride a good enough race on this course? With its great wide open spaces, Newmarket is a very difficult course for an apprentice to ride on. For different reasons, Brighton and Epsom pose equally severe problems.

Can he ride the type of race suitable for your selection? Accurate timing of a strong late finish is quite difficult, and there are very few apprentices who are able to do this with consistency.

An added complication is that some apprentices who do know how to ride this kind of race leave their finish too late, in an attempt to play to the gallery. Surprisingly this is a more common fault than making the run too early and not being able to hold on till the line.

What about apprentice handicaps? I don't think I have ever found a betting opportunity in this sort of race, and I think if I did I would tread warily. The danger would lie in the less skilled apprentices not being able to keep their mounts out of each other's way.

Now we have considered every factor involved—when should we have a bet?

CHAPTER EIGHT
Betting to Win

A 'punter' sets out to make a large amount of money with no effort from a small outlay. Tempted by the ever increasing array of weird but not very wonderful bets devised by the bookmaker—the Yankee, the Union Jack and so on—he has no chance of making his betting pay in the long run. The bookmakers give the very occasional win of this kind the full blast of their publicity machine—'Bristol widow wins £20,287 for a 10p stake'. How often do you hear the betting shop punters lament—*'I would have won £200 if only that third horse had come up.'*

How many punters keep a record of their bets and their betting expenses (newspapers etc.)? If they did, they would realise what their hobby was costing. If you bet say £2 every racing day, this means you will lay out £600 each year on bets alone. If you buy a racing paper, even the most inexpensive (the *Racing Post*) will cost you £140.40 a year (1989 prices). Bookmakers estimate that the average punter retains about 80% of his stake over a long series of bets (in my experience this is a considerable overestimate)—in our example, this would mean a loss of £120 per year on your bets and a total cost of £260.40.

One bet I feel is a certainty—I bet you didn't realise it cost you so much!

If you aim to be a serious backer, consider the Turf like any other investment, keeping a record of your bets and *all* your expenses. Adopt a coolly realistic attitude to your results—but don't tell anyone else. You often hear of someone boasting of winning £100 for a 5p accumulator—but how often do they tell you about the losers?

That is the affliction of the small punter—at the other end of the social scale is a more pathetic affliction: the wealthy person who boasts about his losses, like the Chicago millionaires in the 1880s who vied with each other for the size of dollar bill they could use to light their cigars. At Royal Ascot and Goodwood particularly I have heard 'society' people boast how much they have lost during the course of the meeting.

Most punters do not keep a record of their bets. If they did they would realise how much they were losing, and it would shock them into adopting a more analytical approach to their betting. Perhaps they need the reassurance of not knowing how much they have lost, but the first step towards success in anything is **to be realistic.**

Rule number one, therefore: keep a record of your bets. Not only will this give you a realistic idea of how well you are doing, but you can also use your record to improve your technique.

For example, in 1986 after backing KING'S HEAD at Goodwood (see ch 10) I was very puzzled to see him lose quite convincingly. I thought it might be to do with the fact that although he had run well in a very high-class reliable handicap (the **Royal Hunt Cup**) he had never actually won a handicap. So I checked through my records for the previous ten years and found that if I had avoided all similar cases, I would have eliminated numerous losers and only one winner. **If I hadn't kept records this would not have been possible.**

I also find it a good idea to write down **before** each race you are seriously considering, a brief statement of your reasons for making your selection. Not only will this be invaluable for purposes of analysis, it will get you out of one of the worst habits of the small punter—the 'I would have had' habit. How often do you hear this phrase in a betting shop **after** the race is over: 'I would have had the winner if...', or its variants 'I thought of...' and 'I should of...'

But if you are new to racing, I hear you say: '"Investment"—you must be joking! What about the "glorious uncertainty" of the Turf—horses don't run like machines—it's a mug's game.'

In fact, while not machines, horses do run with incredible consistency. **Given similar conditions** they very often run to within 3 feet of their previous performance against each other in a 1m race—a margin of 0.05%. Horse racing, particularly handicap racing, follows a very stable pattern—compare this to the unpredictable fluctuations of exchange rates, interest rates, and political calamities which bedevil the Stock Exchange—'Black Monday', October 1987 being the most notable recent case.

If you follow my recommendations carefully, it is perfectly possible to make a profit of 50% on outlay, after expenses. Even in the exceptionally good years of 1986 and 1987, very few Stock Exchange investors would be able to improve on this result even if they did not have to pay Capital Gains tax. **If you bet on course, there is no tax at all on racing.**

Don't be greedy! It's much more realistic to lay out £1000 and aim to win £500, than to lay out £100 and aim for £500. In fact, this is a good test of the numerous systems which advertise in the sporting press. Take a look through these adverts and see how many tell you the rate of return to outlay on the bets they suggest. You will find any number of extravagant claims for 'winners at 33–1' and none at all for 'losers at 33–1'. The only useful criteria are either the return/outlay ratio or winners/selections ratio.

Like the skilled Stock Exchange investor, the investor on the Turf has a long-term strategy based on research and patience. Even the best operator can go through a period of weeks of backing losers. The key question is, How long can this period last before you are finished? **The average punter thinks of making a profit on the day, we should be thinking in terms of the season. Even some of the most successful backers have been known to have a losing season, yet recover their losses in the following season.**

Concentration and patience are the two most powerful weapons in the armoury of the professional backer.

Concentrate on a small number of races at the best meetings; wait for the opportunity where everything is in your favour. Don't fritter away money just to be sociable or on a fancy 'just for the crack'—if you can cut out these bets, and concentrate on betting only when you really are confident about your selection, then you will improve your winning ratio considerably.

Professional backers score over the average punter in two ways: as a rule, their overall percentage of winners is higher; and they have a much more rational approach to backing their selections.

In my view, the latter is actually as, if not more important than making the selections. If you followed any form ratings you would have a winning ratio of 30%. I don't think it's realistic to be able to expect to raise this above 40%, and am quite happy to settle for around 35%.

I doubt if any professional backer has done much better than around 40% over a long period although I am quite prepared to believe that many punters do in fact have a higher strike rate. **The crucial difference lies in the professionals' approach to betting in terms of strategy and staking.** By this I do not simply mean a logical approach to betting, although this is important. What is more important is a psychologically sound approach which will enable you to bet for a long time—you will only win in the long run and you need a system to equip you to do so.

Therefore, it makes very sound psychological sense before you place a bet to ask yourself: how will I feel if I lose this bet? If you think that it would lead you to have second thoughts about betting again, then ask yourself, how much would I be prepared to lose? There are no absolutes here: you should certainly never bet more than you can afford to lose, but some people will worry over losing £5, to others a loss of £500 will cause no concern, whatever their circumstances. In fact, you must try to make the most of your losses—learn from your mistakes and analyse them.

Why should you expect instant success in racing? Nobody expects it in any other area of investment—in the Stock Exchange people study and invest very carefully for years before they make a success of it.

Don't go away with the idea that there is a category of people on the Turf, the 'insiders' who can make large sums from their privileged access to stable secrets. It is true that trainers and owners have inside information you don't have—but on the other hand they don't have such information year in year out. This is especially true of the smaller trainers who may have a good set of handicappers they can beat the book with this year, but may have to wait another two or three years before they are in the same position again.

Even if you have 'inside information' about a particular horse, there are other people with inside information about other horses—and who is to decide which is right?

Most people can't rid themselves of the James Bond image of a gambler: big hat, big cigar and a retinue of hangers-on. Whether he wins or loses thousands, he is always ready with some super-cool remark. All the **successful** gamblers I've ever met or read about have been nothing like that, although I've met plenty of **un**successful ones who have lived up to this image. Even such a consistently successful gambler as Alex Bird has written that he worries himself sick before he has a bet, and no-one could take more trouble over studying form.

One of the most difficult things at the beginning is to ignore the reactions of your fellow punters. Say you get really interested in studying form, no matter what approach you follow, the one advocated in this book or some other.

You give up all the 'mug' bets, the chancy doubles, the hopeful accumulators— and yet after all that your first two or three bets go down. You imagine the taunts of your friends—'All that studying form and you couldn't pick a winner'—and you feel foolish!

My advice—persevere! At least you **know** that the average punter can **never** win in the long run—perhaps you won't do all that much better, but you will have learned a great deal more about racing and you'll get more enjoyment out of it.

Once we have made this mental adjustment, what is a logical approach to betting? My logical rules are very simple and do not require a degree in pure mathematics to understand—just simple arithmetic.

The main rule is that your estimate of the chances of the horse should remain totally independent of the odds offered by the bookmaker. In fact, it is a very good idea to make your selection without looking at the odds on offer by the bookmakers. Punters often scan the form lines and refer to the betting 'show' and are too much influenced by the latter. **You should make your selection—and the odds should only determine how much you should stake, not your selection.**

Any system which involves backing favourites, first, second, third or any combination whatsoever, is not based on the **objective** chances the horse has of winning. It is not necessarily even based on the generally held view of the horse's chances of winning. Very often a horse will start at a short price because the **bookmaker thinks that the public is likely to think that the horse will win** ie this is a defensive ploy by the bookmaker to ensure that he does not offer a price to the public which will prove so popular that he will not be able to balance his books.

Nor does a short price necessarily reflect 'inside information' ie that the stable is confident of the horse's winning and has forced the price down by weight of money.

In the first place, if a *coup* is being planned, a 'dark' horse will probably start at a longer price than the favourites.

Secondly, fluctuations in the prices offered are as likely to reflect the bookmaker's manipulation of the odds as a real 'gamble'. Most commonly, the bookmaker shortens the odds, gullible punters think that the horse is 'fancied' and rush in. A less common practice nowadays is where an on course bookmaker 'knocks out' a horse by lengthening its odds, so as to give a favourable S.P. which his associates can take advantage of in off-course betting. **In neither case will the horse run faster or slower as a result of the bookmaker's strategy—your estimate must be based on the former rather than the latter.**

Simple arithmetic shows that it is very bad policy to back a horse at a short price. If your selection is at 5–4 against, it means you have to have a 50% success rate to make a small percentage profit; to make a reasonable profit of 35%, your strike rate has to be 60%. If you had a series of 10 bets of £10 each, the results would be as follows:

ODDS	SUCCESS RATE	RETURN ON £100 (10 BETS AT £10)
5 – 4	5 out of 10 +	£12.50
5 – 4	6 out of 10 +	£35.00
5 – 4	7 out of 10 +	£57.50

If you must take short prices, can I convince you that betting odds-on (sometimes called 'buying money' although 'throwing money away' would be more apt) is suicidal? For example, if you bet at 5–4 on, you have to have more than 5 winners out of 10 to break even; if you have 6 winners out of 10, the rate of return on your 'investment' (assuming that you bet on course and do not pay tax) is 8%—that is not much higher than a good building society account, and I know which I think is a safer bet. To get anywhere near the kind of rate of return we are aiming at, you have to get select an incredible 8 winners out of 10 (44% return).

ODDS	SUCCESS RATE	RETURN ON £100 (10 BETS AT £10)
4 – 5	6 out of 10 +	£8.00
4 – 5	7 out of 10 +	£26.00
4 – 5	8 out of 10 +	£44.00

Even if you were to operate at only a 30% strike rate, if you restrict your bets to 7–2 upwards, you will make a profit of at least 35%; whereas at the shorter price (6–4) you would will make a loss of 25%.

ODDS	SUCCESS RATE	RETURN ON £100 (10 BETS AT £10)
7 – 2	3 out of 10 +	£35.00
6 – 4	3 out of 10 –	£25.00

It follows logically that you shouldn't chase the money ie bet more if the price shortens. In fact, you should consider doing precisely the opposite—if the price

lengthens, and there is no obvious reason for it which you can see eg the horse is sweating, has gone down to post badly—have the courage of your convictions and increase your stake. It's still the same horse, and in your judgement has still the same chance.

While it is true that most punters have little idea of value for money, some like the phrase. Punters are often advised to look at several horses with a roughly equal chance. If there are two horses, one of which is − 4 in your handicap and is offered at 4–1, the other is − 2 and offered at 2–1, they will say that the 4–1 horse is the 'value' bet.

This is quite illogical. The − 4 horse is not well in, and should not be backed at all, whatever the odds. The length of the odds cannot in any way compensate for the weakness of his chances. In my view if a horse which is − 2 in your book runs in 2 races, in which he is 7–4 in one and 7–2 in the other, then he is a value bet only in the second race.

The first rule of a logical approach to betting, therefore, is never to bet in handicaps at odds of less than 7–2.

. The second rule is to work out a sensible system of staking. Even if your proportion of winners is low, a good system can at least help you reduce your losses. Most punters do exactly the opposite of what is logical—they spend their winnings and chase their losses. Instead, you should learn to cut your losses and capitalise on your winnings. Every investor, on racing or the Stock Exchange, has winning and losing streaks. There is nothing mystical in this.

A system which attempts to chase losses can rapidly end up with you betting in large sums in an attempt to get back the relatively small sum you lost at the start. Even when these systems have some arithmetical sense to them, they completely ignore the psychological dimension. When you are on a losing streak, it is very easy to lose confidence altogether. If you are betting increasingly large sums which seem to be getting out of control and you still lose, the natural thing to do is to give up altogether. Perhaps the ideal mathematical punter would have continued and recovered the stake; a real person will give up and lose heavily.

Whatever system you use, begin with a bank of say £2000 which you are prepared in advance to lose completely. Many professional backers at the beginning of their careers get 'wiped out' completely. This may happen two or three times before you really begin to be successful. This shows the value of keeping a record of all your bets—you can go back and try to find out where you went wrong.

How should you use your bank? I think that there are only two staking systems worth following. The first is the simplest and doesn't merit the name of 'staking system'. It is to have a level stake bet on every selection. It is more important for what you don't do ie increasing stakes after a loser. The second is more sensible, because it is based on the principle of capitalising on your winnings and cutting your losses. It works in two versions: a simple and a complicated.

In the simple version, when your bank has gone up or down by a given percentage (say 50%) you stake your bets as percentages of your new bank. If you have lost 5 bets at £100, then your new bank is £500 and your stake at 1/10th is £50; conversely, if you have had 5 winners, your new bank is £1500 and your stake at 1/10th if £150.

The more complicated staking system responds more directly to your success or failure. Divide this into 10 units, here £200 each. For your first investment, bet £200. Say it loses, your bank is now (assuming no tax) £1800. On your next investment, invest 1/10th ie £180. If you have three consecutive losers, you will have lost £442, a considerable difference from the £600 you would have lost using

69

level stakes.

If you win, say a 7–2 bet, put the £700 into the bank, and make your next bet 1/10 of your bank, ie £270. If you have winning and losing streaks like every other investor I know, this will minimise your losses and maximise your profits. More important, it will safeguard your confidence during the inevitable losing runs.

Before you start on any system, I think you should do a few calculations, based on what you consider would be the **worst possible outcome**. Most, if not all, of the staking systems advertised on the sporting press only apply to favourable outcomes or a favourable distribution of winners.

In calculating the worst possible case, you have to give more attention to psychology than to mathematics—ie how will I feel in the middle of a losing run? Let's consider some examples. I assume that the worst case is 30% winners; and that as I never bet under 7/2, all the selections are at 7/2.

If I bet on level stakes, then whatever the distribution of winners I will always make 3.5 points on a 10 point outlay. To make this clear, assume that 1 point = £100. Now what happens if the losers come in a sequence—to have 7 consecutive losers is pretty demoralising. Consider the two following sequences:

L	L	L	L	L	L	L	W	W	W
900	810	729	656	591	532	479	643	867	1178
−100	−90	−81	−73	−65	−59	−53	+165	+224	+303

It is worth looking at the differences in some detail. In my proportional system you will have laid out £718 and won £171, a return of 24%; in level staking, you will have laid out £1000 and won £350, a return of 35%. On paper, level staking looks much better—but now ask yourself, how will you feel coming up to the 8th bet after 7 consecutive losers? On level stake betting, you will have lost £700 and about to stake £100; on my system, £468 and about to stake £47.

Furthermore, if you increase your bank only after 50% profit, you will be still operating with a £100 stake; in my system, your bank will be £1170, ie 17% higher, and you will be operating a stake of £117. If the next series of 10 bets is more successful, then you will be better placed to make a better percentage.

Now for another sequence.

W	L	L	L	L	L	L	L	W	W
1350	1215	1094	1985	887	799	720	647	873	1178
+350	−135	−121	−109	−98	−88	−80	−72	+226	+305

On a level stake system, you will have laid out £1000 and won £350, as usual 35%; here you will have laid out £955 and won £178 ie a return of 18.6%. But on your 9th bet, after 7 consecutive losers, you will be £450 down and laying out £100; in my system, you will be £353 down, and laying out £65. Again you will be going forward into your next series with a higher bank.

The system I adopt is a variant of the above. That is, for a 7–2 bet I use 10% of my bank, for a 4–1 bet 12½% and for each half point in the betting up to maximum of 6–1 increments of 2½%. Over the years I have in fact found that winners are not in fact evenly distributed, they in fact tend to come in at the longer prices. Even if they were evenly distributed, one would be better off than a level percentage, and would only be worse off if unevenly distributed in favour of the lower odds.

If you run this as a continuous system over a period of time the bank will build up substantially. Assume that you are able to make 50% profit on your bank each year. Beginning with £2000 the progression looks like this:

End of Year	One	Two	Three	Four	Five
	3000	4500	6600	9900	14850

Whatever type of racing you are interested in, providing you follow a consistent principle of selection, you should be able to achieve a success rate of 30%. Betting strategy is the the key to making racing pay.

It can be summarised in the following rules:

1. Always keep a record of your bets.
2. Concentrate on a small number of races at the best meetings; wait for the opportunity when everything is in your favour.
3. NEVER EVER bet odds-on.
4. Wait till you can get odds of 7–2 or better against your selection.
5. Don't chase your losses.
6. Cut your losses and play up your winnings.

CHAPTER NINE
Racing Through the Season

In this chapter I will look at the general pattern of the racing season, which hardly varies from year to year. The Flat racing season is usually 32 weeks long (see the Calendar of the Racing Year at the end of this chapter). For maximum effectiveness the reader is advised to concentrate on the high season, from the Epsom Derby meeting in the first week of June to the Ayr Western meeting in the third week of September (weeks 11–26).

This chapter describes the different techniques which are appropriate to the different parts of the season. It should be read in conjunction with chapter 6 'Key Races', for further information.

1. From the beginning of the season to the Epsom Derby meeting.

In my opinion, it is quite difficult to find many worthwhile opportunities during this period. **For the first few weeks there is little or no form to go on, and it is extremely difficult to evaluate the form of these races. The going is often soft and subject to rapid changes; fitness is at a premium; and horses which have been hurdling in this country or racing at Cagnes often have an inestimable advantage. Even if you have a horse with apparently reasonable form it is always vulnerable to the first time out winner.**

In these circumstances, races are often won by a wide, hence meaningless margin. Next time out the fit runaway winner fresh from a hurdling campaign which has trounced a field of elderly and unfit hopefuls, may meet completely different opposition, with results gratifying only to the bookmakers.

Following the form shown in the previous season is always risky—this is particularly true of three year olds. Many horses which have shown promise in their first season completely fail to 'train on'—this applies not only to the numerous classic hopes which bite the dust in their third year, but also to good nursery winners.

In any case, these horses are likely to have been fairly assessed and will now be anchored high in the handicap. If they have still retained their ability, it will take several runs down the field to 'work off' this high weight.

Your first rule must be not to bet during this period. If you must bet on something, I understand from greyhound racing friends that the April–June period produces very reliable results. If you must bet on horses during this period, at least bet lightly so as to minimise your losses!

Most of the early season handicaps, such as the Lincoln (week 1 Doncaster) and the Newbury Spring Cup (week 4), are a real trap for the punter. It is also true that the quality of horses entered for the better early season handicaps has declined in recent years, especially at the first Epsom meeting. The City and Suburban Handicap (10f) and the Great Metropolitan Handicap (formerly 2m 2f now reduced to 12f) are now very ordinary handicaps indeed, which do not attract good class horses.

During this period, my rules for class (see ch five) do not apply so rigorously and some quite moderate handicaps at lower grade courses attract horses of a reasonable calibre and good form from them can be surprisingly confirmed at higher grade courses.

Nevertheless there are a few genuine opportunities during this part of the season and some useful pointers for later in the season. In sequence, they are as follows (refer to Key Races, ch 6 for details).

The Kempton Easter meeting is usually run on soft ground but when the going is good, the Rosebery Handicap is worth considering, and some of the other handicaps at Kempton can provide pointers for early season winners (STATEN ISLAND 1988). This is also a good time to get your eye in for watching races.

The first Newmarket meeting (the Craven Meeting) begins in the 4th week. Although the going is usually good here, we still do not have enough good class form to warrant a sensible bet, but these races must be watched for pointers to the future. This applies with even greater force to the Ascot meeting (the **Victoria Cup**) and the Newmarket Guineas meeting.

Newmarket form ranks very high throughout the season, but up to the Royal Ascot meeting it ranks highest of all. The 10f Across the Flat course at Newmarket is a very stiff test, and a winner of a handicap race there in good style can be followed with confidence (MOON MADNESS 1986).

May begins with the Chester meeting. This is of interest to the student of the Classics, but I avoid it: the flat circular course one mile in circumference, with its straight run in of only one furlong is quite unlike any other British flat course, and produces extremely misleading form.

The York May meeting can very occasionally provide an opportunity in the sprint races, but although the form book is beginning to fill up I still find it sensible to avoid this meeting. Even in May there are still upsets in going, and the backer should be particularly wary of York in this respect.

During this part of the season, I pay great attention to race times. I have explained elsewhere that by themselves one cannot build a system on them, but a handicapper who records a good time (*Raceform* speed rating of 65+) in this period should be given serious consideration. However, you will not find many such horses (MERDON MELODY 1987).

2. From the Epsom Derby meeting to the Ayr Western meeting.

Our time has come! The patience which I hope you have shown during the first weeks of the season avoiding bad bets should now pay off. There is now an increasing amount of reliable form in the book; the going tends to be consistent in 9 seasons out of 10; and most handicaps are well contested and provide good lines of form.

Even during this period, it is unrealistic to expect a good betting opportunity every day, or even every week. A look at the Calendar of the Racing Year shows that there are several 'blank' weeks. For example, the weeks before and after Royal Ascot are usually rather quiet. But the reader will soon find that he works to a rhythm—there may be no good opportunities for two or three weeks—and you will then find that there are two or three in as many days.

The Epsom Derby meeting has several high-grade handicaps. Although the quality of the contestants often leaves something to be desired, it is usually possible to find one or two sound opportunities. At this meeting, I do not find it necessary to apply the class criterion as rigorously as it must be applied later in the season. Winners can go up in grade and come from a lower grade course and still win. **However, because of the peculiar nature of the course, it does not offer any pointers to the future.**

Royal Ascot brings high-class handicappers into play for the first time. It is possible, but difficult to find handicap winners here. It is no more difficult, at any rate, than it is to find the winners of the two year old races which provide shocks every year. More importantly, unless the going is soft which happens only rarely (three times in the last 15 years), we should be able to find two or three pointers to good winners later in the season.

We now have reliable form lines, in most years the going is consistently good, and races well contested—this is when patience in the first third of the season should pay off handsomely. The class test must be applied rigorously—it is rare to find a horse winning at a lower class meeting able to succeed in a higher class.

3. From the Ayr Western meeting to the end of the season.

The last 5 weeks of the season offer the opposite problem to the first 11 weeks. There is now a surfeit of form: most horses will be correctly handicapped, and you will frequently find that several horses are grouped very closely in the handicap. **It is less likely that trainer will attempt to exploit a fast-improving horse at this stage of the season—with one exception: nurseries, ie handicaps for two year olds.**

Although in recent years we have had a series of fine autumns, rapid changes of going similar to those in the first part of the season do happen. We should be careful about courses such as York, where this can happen quickly and unpredictably. I find it a good rule during this part of the season to confine myself to the three meetings at Newmarket—races are well contested and of a good standard; and there are not the enormous fields that one gets especially at the Midland meetings such as Leicester or Warwick with their air of desperation as trainers with second rank handicappers struggle to find a race for them before the season is over.

A repeated word of warning about Newmarket—avoid the Cesarewitch and the Cambridgeshire: the former because it is run over a distance (2m2f) for which there are few handicappers, the latter because its distance (9f) requires an unusual combination of speed and stamina tested by few other races.

CALENDAR OF THE RACING YEAR

(In brackets I give the number of days and handicap races for important meetings, followed by the names of the important handicaps)

WEEK
01   DONCASTER (Lincoln Handicap)
02

APRIL
03   KEMPTON—Easter meeting (Rosebery Handicap)
04   NEWMARKET—Craven Meeting; NEWBURY (Spring Cup)
05   EPSOM—Spring meeting (City and Suburban); SANDOWN (Esher Cup)
06   ASCOT—(Victoria Cup); NEWMARKET—Spring Meeting (Guineas)

MAY
07
08   YORK (David Dixon Sprint)
09   REDCAR (Zetland Gold Cup)
10   NEWMARKET (10f A.F.handicap); SANDOWN (Whitsun Cup)

74

JUNE

11 EPSOM—Derby meeting (3 days—6 races)
12 YORK; NEWBURY (**Summer Cup**)
13 ROYAL ASCOT (3 days—5 races: **Royal Hunt Cup; Bessborough Handicap King George V Handicap; Wokingham Handicap; Britannia Handicap**)
14 NEWCASTLE (**Gosforth Park Cup**); NEWMARKET (1 day—2 races)

JULY

15 HAYDOCK (**Old Newton Cup**); SANDOWN (2 days—5 races)
16 NEWMARKET—July meeting (3 days—5 races: **Bunbury Cup**); YORK (2 days—6 races)
17 NEWMARKET (1 day—2 races)
18 SANDOWN (2 days—1 race); ASCOT (2 days—1 race (sprint))
19 GOODWOOD (5 days—8 races: **Extel Handicap**); SANDOWN (1 day—2 races)

AUGUST

20
21
22 RIPON (**Great St. Wilfrid**) YORK (3 days—7 races); NEWMARKET days—4 races)
23 SANDOWN (2 days—2 races)

SEPTEMBER

24 YORK (2 days—4 races)
25 DONCASTER—St. Leger meeting (4 days—7 races; **Portland Cup**)
26 AYR—Western Meeting (**Ayr Gold Cup**); SANDOWN (2 days—1 race); NEWBURY (**Autumn Cup**)
27 ASCOT (2 days—1 race)

OCTOBER

28 NEWMARKET (4 days—4 races; **Cambridgeshire**)
29 YORK (3 days—8 races) ASCOT (2 days—1 race)
30 NEWMARKET (3 days—8 races; **Cesarewitch**)
31 DONCASTER (2 days—3 races)

NOVEMBER

32 NEWMARKET (2 days—2 races); DONCASTER (2 days—2 races)

CHAPTER TEN

A typical season: 1986

To show my method in operation, this chapter deals with an average season, 1986. The Race numbers refer to the Official Jockey Club record which are those in *Raceform Note-Book, the Raceform Flat Annual,* and the *Raceform Handicap Book*; the handicap grade is adjusted to the current system of 0–140. Thus a race listed as 0–35 in the form book for 1986 is 0–75 in the current system, and is shown as such in this chapter.

22 March Doncaster Lincoln Handicap (Race 43: 8f 0–115)
This race provided a surprise as usual. The winner (K BATTERY) had always struck me as a 10f horse, with a good turn of foot. But the strong headwind made this race a test of stamina, so his burst of speed was brought into play to win quite well.

This win would put him out of the handicap class—for the rest of the season he found himself in the unfortunate position of being too highly rated for handicaps, yet not quite good enough to win a Group 3 race.

31 March Kempton Rosebery Handicap (Race 89: 10f 0–110)
More often than not (10 out of the last 15 years) the Easter meeting is run on soft ground. The first important handicap of the season, this race sometimes includes a horse which was improving at the end of the previous season. This year there was no entry of that kind today. The race was won quite well by NEBRIS, fit from hurdling.

For the first month of the season, it seemed to be rain almost every day. Even the first Newmarket meeting was run on yielding to soft, producing surprises and no noteworthy winners.

22 April Epsom City and Suburban Handicap (Race 325: 10f 0–100)
The first day of the Epsom spring meeting was run on heavy ground. This race used to be one of the season's leading handicaps and very competitive, but now it is a run-of-the-mill 0–100. NEBRIS was among the top weights, but I couldn't be confident that he would repeat his win in the **Rosebery** (see 31 March above)—but he did, with something in hand.

30 April Ascot Victoria Cup (Race 412: 7f 0–115)
This is often a useful pointer to races at this specialist distance, but today's field seemed rather sub-standard. It was won by the 4 year old READY WIT in quite good style. This was considerably in advance of anything he had done before. In 1985 READY WIT had won a seller at the Doncaster St. Leger meeting and then been down the field in an 8f Newbury handicap.

He could be considered for one of the key 7f races in this going, if not too highly penalised by the handicapper for his win. As it turned out, he did not run in a suitable race in 1986.

2 May Newmarket Ely Handicap (Race 441: 6f 0–110 3-y.o)
The first good going this season—and the first really impressive winner— MERDON MELODY. As a two year old he had won an ordinary 5f plate at Sandown, and then run unplaced. However, his time for good going (*Raceform*

figure, 49) was not particularly outstanding, and although he had beaten a largish field, I could not be sure of the quality of his victory.

5 May Kempton The Jubilee Handicap (Race 472: 8f 0–115)
This race was won in really commanding style by PENNINE WALK. Carrying 9–11 he would now be too high for handicaps, but it was reassuring to be reminded of the style of victory one is always looking for. One can watch a month of races without seeing it and wonder if there are still any horses around with this quality.

READY WIT ran in this race with an 8lbs penalty—not only was this too much in my opinion (in my book he was − 4), but the going was now fast, and this race was 8f. In these circumstances he could not be backed. At 11–1 he ran well down the field, and didn't do anything in his other two races during the season.

The fast going at Kempton was an exception—elsewhere the soft going continued well into May, and tested my reserves of patience.

26 May Redcar Zetland Gold Cup (Race 776: 10f 0–100)
A rather uninspiring field for this once well contested handicap. It included a typical Luca Cumani 'dark horse', BARLEY BILL, which had already won 4 minor races and was still very much an unknown quantity.

He was, however, still a 3 year old and I thought it was trying him rather highly running him against older horses at this stage of the season. As it happens, we will never know how good he was at this stage, as during the race he was struck into and finished lame. He did not run later in the season nor in 1987.

The race was won quite well by a filly, FORWARD RALLY, which had won a 0–75 at Beverley last time out.

26 May Sandown The Whitsun Cup (Race 790: 8f 0–110)
This race often turns up some good performers. It was won by SIYAH KALEM, who hit the front at the distance and ran on strongly. Trained by John Dunlop, I had good hopes that he could be placed to win another race, perhaps at Epsom or Ascot, if not too highly penalised for this win.

31 May Newmarket The Holsten Export Lager Handicap (Race 845: 10f 0–100)
The most promising performance yet from our point of view. The race was won very easily by MOON MADNESS. Here he took the lead 2f out and won by 5 lengths almost in a canter, indeed with almost embarrassing ease—in our view at least 14 lbs in hand. This is the sort of victory that causes the official handicapper nightmares!

On his only previous outing as a 3 year old he had won a weakly-contested maiden race at Salisbury; and he had run green in his only two year old race. The 10f Across the Flat races at Newmarket are a very reliable test of a horse. A winner of such a race in this style has a good future—I hoped he would be entered for a handicap at Epsom or Royal Ascot.

5 June—8 June The Epsom Derby Meeting
The weather seemed to have changed for the better, and going was good for the whole 4 days. But because so many previous races had been run on soft going, there was little form to go on.

7 June Haydock Stones Best Bitter Handicap (Race 981: 10f 131y 0–110)
The target for MOON MADNESS was not the Epsom Derby meeting, but here—I thought he would be suited by the slightly extra distance, but as I never bet on races of this distance at Haydock I regretfully passed him over. Not

surprisingly, in rather an ordinary field he was set to carry 9–13, but he won in the same tremendous style as he had at Newmarket. I hoped that he would now go for Royal Ascot.

As usual the period between the Derby and the Ascot meeting fell rather flat. Although I hadn't found a really good opportunity yet, I was confident that if the Royal Ascot meeting was held in good weather, there was every prospect of a profitable summer.

18 June Royal Ascot Royal Hunt Cup (Race 1144: 8f 0–115)

Fortunately, the going was good here, and the racing provided some useful pointers to later events—things were beginning to take shape. One has to be extra-cautious in betting on this race, but it often highlights future winners.

So it proved today. SIYAH KALEM was in the race, but I thought he would not be able to carry a 7lbs penalty over this stiff course. However, PATRIACH from the same stable, ran on courageously to win and I thought he could well repeat the performance if suitably placed. The 4 year old PATRIACH had only won one handicap before, as a 3 year old (a lowly 0–75 at Leicester in the 1985 backend), after 2 undistinguished races in his first season. Clearly he was on the upgrade.

KING'S HEAD on his first race this season ran on well into third place. As a three-year-old he had won one stakes, and then run down the field in the Cambridgeshire. He had not run as a 2 year old. I thought he could certainly be placed to win a handicap.

18 June Royal Ascot Bessborough Handicap (Race 1147: 12f 0–115)

Unfortunately, this usually very informative race was a real rough house, with half a dozen horses involved in a scrimmage close home. CONVINCED was awarded the race, but could not be included in my calculations. In his next race, the **Great Yorkshire Handicap** (Race 2250: 12f 0–100) at the York August meeting, he was a well-beaten 6th.

19 June Royal Ascot King George V Handicap (Race 1153: (12f 0–110 3-y.o)

At last our patience was rewarded. Because of the changeable going during the first 13 weeks of the season I had refrained from betting—many punters probably lost a packet as there were numerous form upsets. Now I had a golden opportunity and was ready to strike. MOON MADNESS who had won easily at Haydock (Race 981) since I noted him was well in here with +2 as, the handicapper still hadn't caught up with him. He opened at 5–1 and SP at 4–1. He won readily by 5 lengths, and later in the season went on to win the St.Leger.

20 June Royal Ascot The Wokingham Handicap (Race 1156: 6f 0–115)

This race is one of the hottest sprint handicaps of the year. It is very hard to find the winner, but year after year horses which run well close up can win next time out if suitably placed. The 28 runners ensured a terrific pace (*Raceform* speed figure, 72) and 2 lengths covered the first 5, with the second MANIMSTAR, a 6 year old, beaten a neck, running particularly well.

He had won 3 handicaps in 1985 (including 2 at Newmarket over 6f), seeming to run his best races when covered up. He seemed to me to be a tricky ride rather than ungenuine, as some commentators had claimed.

In the same race, the 4 year old ROTHERFIELD GREYS was drawn high, and raced virtually alone when the field divided. He ran on well for four furlongs. He could not be on my short list, as he was too far out of the frame, but I decided to look him up for future reference. He had won two 0–75 apprentice handicaps this season, at Warwick and Edinburgh, rather a come down from his early days as a 2 year old. After his first race, it was thought he might become one of the leading northern horses of his generation—he was only 1¼ lengths behind the winner in the Group 3 July Stakes at Newmarket. As a 3 year old he made no impact in his two stakes races. Perhaps he was finding his level as a sprint handicapper.

20 June Royal Ascot Britannia Handicap (Race 1158: 8f 0–110 3-y.o)

DALLAS won this race very impressively. He was a typical Luca Cumani 'dark horse'. He did not run as a 2 year old, but won his previous (second) race, a Brighton stakes, by 1½ lengths. I couldn't possibly consider him, but I thought that the rule which allows a horse to be entered for a handicap after only two races puts the official handicapper in an impossible position.

He won by 1 length here, though it could have been 10, in a very fast time (*Raceform* speed figure, 87). I couldn't see him running in handicaps again, but after one race in a stakes he won the Cambridgeshire—an excellent performance for a three year old, but not one of our handicaps.

Although he had no chance with the winner, NAVARZATO, winner of his only two races as a two year old, a stakes and a nursery, ran well and went into the notebook.

My operations now focus on the Class One courses and the top-class races at the other courses. Whichever section of the handicap racing scene you prefer, the most favourable part of the season is now beginning.

28 June Newmarket Barclays Bank Handicap (Race 1330: 6f 0–100)

MANIMSTAR was out again quickly after his good run in the Wokingham. +1 on our reckoning, twice a winner over course and distance, he was as near a handicap certainty as one could ever get. His main rival was the filly PERFECT TIMING 1 length behind (rec 6lbs) in the Wokingham—here they met on identical terms. MANIMSTAR came with a strong run with just under a furlong to go and won by 3 lengths, with an excellent *Raceform* speed figure of 82. I considered he could win one more race before the handicapper got his measure.

4 July Sandown Wayfoong Handicap (Race 1435: 8f 0–100 3-y.o)

In this race I saw the best burst of acceleration so far this season. AVENTINO was held up, and came with a strong burst at the furlong pole to win by 1½ lengths, but in my view with at least 7lbs in hand.

Bought in from a seller at the end of the previous season, he had already won 3 handicaps. He was trained by John Sutcliffe, who really knows how to place this kind of horse. In 1984 his COURTING SEASON had won this race with a similar burst of speed, and gone on to win an 8f handicap at the Newmarket July meeting. I hoped that AVENTINO would be an action replay.

5 July Haydock The Old Newton Cup (Race 1428: 12f 0–115)

This is the only race I ever consider at this course over this distance, if it attracts an Ascot winner. This year it did not, being won by RAKAPOSHI KING. He won in great style by 5 lengths, but on past form he is more a 14f horse and would probably be aimed at the Ebor Handicap.

8 July Newmarket The Bunbury Cup (Race 1493: 7f 0–115)

On to my favourite meeting of the year: there is plenty of form by now, some high class handicaps, and usually fine weather. This is a good race for us, especially if contested by the winner of the Victoria Cup or the Hunt Cup. Here PATRIACH though carrying a 7lbs penalty was rated by me at −2 in a competitive field. I usually look for a + figure, but this race is a favourable placing for a Royal Hunt Cup winner. PATRIACH went off at 6–1 and won very convincingly.

9 July Newmarket The Duke of Cambridge Handicap (Race 1500: 10f 0–110 3-y.o)
This race is a good illustration of my views about Key Races. Although it is for high grade handicappers, run at a prestigious course, and offers good prize money, somehow it never attracts an improving 3 year old or one that is of very high (handicapping) class. You could spend hours agonising over the form books and never come up with a convincing selection. Nor does the winner seem to go on to anything special. This year was no exception.

10 July Newmarket Addison Tools Handicap for 3 year olds (Race 1506: 8f 0–115)
AVENTINO had only a 4 lbs penalty and was therefore +3+ in my handicap. Given the command at the final furlong he simply cantered over this quite competitive field—and at 4–1! He was collared by the handicapper after this, and did not win again in his remaining 3 races.

11 July York The Lin Pac Handicap (Race 1558: 5f 0–110)
I could not find a bet at this meeting. ROTHERFIELD GREYS, which I had looked up after the Wokingham, won in a good time (with a *Raceform* speed figure of 75) by running on strongly and I decided to note him for next time.

12 July York The John Smith's Magnet Cup (Race 1564: 10f 110y 0–115)
This race used to provide a good opportunity fairly often. However, in recent years it does not seem to attract quite the same class of horse. CHAUMIERE won it exactly in the same style as he had in 1985: a strong late burst in the last furlong, but though quite genuine I had never found him reliable and did not include him in the notebook.

As in most seasons there is a fortnight's gap where the racing is of average quality and there was nothing to note. Even the one-day second July meeting at Newmarket and the 2-day Ascot meeting do not offer much for the handicap enthusiast who, like everyone else, is waiting for Goodwood.

29 July Goodwood Stewards Cup (Race 1898: 6f 0–115)
It is very difficult to find the winner of this race. So it proved this year: 20–1 GREEN RUBY had been noted as running quite well this season but only with hindsight could this be said to amount anything. Like the Wokingham, this is a good race for observations—but not this year: four lengths covered the first nine, none of which had anything left to give.

31 July Goodwood Darnley Handicap (Race 1908: 12f 0–110 3-y.o)
For many years, Dick Hern's stable produced with unfailing regularity a certain type of handicapper—late developing, strong, with a good burst of finishing speed (eg TOWN AND COUNTRY 1978; RHYME AND ROYAL 1979; BEDTIME 1983) but these have become rather rare recently.

I thought that on his running here HAUWMAL might be of this type. Disappointing as a 2 year old, he had won a stakes this season and ran on in fine style here. I hoped he would not be aimed at a race at the Newbury August meeting, as Goodwood winners have a poor record there over the years. Unfortunately, HAUWMAL turned out to be rather one paced and did not win again in 1986; in 1987 he became one of those unfortunate animals too heavily weighted for handicaps but not good enough to win a Group race.

1 August Goodwood Extel Handicap (Race 1916: 10f 0–115 3-y.o)
This is the season's top handicap for 3 year olds over this distance. It contained

its usual quota of dark horses which had won modest plates by unassessable margins. The winner, CHINOISERIE, had won a modest handicap at Yarmouth and then been twice second in Windsor stakes. He quickened well but the winners of this handicap usually move out of handicaps, as he did returning here in September to win a stakes.

NAVARZATO was in this race but this is a handicap to avoid. He ran very disappointingly, being well down the field. In fact he did not win in 1986 and did not appear at all in 1987 so something must have gone badly wrong.

2 August Goodwood Racal Chesterfield Cup (Race 1921: 10f 0–115)

My only betting opportunities at the meeting came on the last day, Saturday.

KING'S HEAD who had run well in the Royal Hunt Cup appeared in this race. This is not the race it used to be, and often does not take a great deal of winning. I was not worried about the extra 2 furlongs, and thought him a good bet at +2. I got 7–2 before he was pushed down to 15–8. In the race he was perhaps brought to the front too soon 3 furlongs out, but he did not seem to have any reserves.

Every defeat makes you look more analytically at your selection process. Looking back through his record I realised that he had never won a handicap at all (cf. MANIMSTAR, Race 1330, who though he had not won one this season had done so in previous seasons). This is where the value of keeping good records comes in. I looked through **all** my previous selections and found that it would be a good rule not to back horses which had not previously won a handicap.

As it happened, KING'S HEAD disappointed in his next handicap, over 8f at the York August meeting, and did not appear at all in 1987.

2 August Goodwood Albert Handicap (Race 1923: 6f 0–100)

This is not one of Goodwood's star races, but provided a golden opportunity. MANIMSTAR was well in here (+2 in our ratings) and won comfortably at 6–1. I feared that the handicapper might punish him for this—what else could he do after two such easy wins—and he did.

2 August Newmarket Cardinal Handicap (Race 1959: 10f 0–100)

The August meetings here are the weakest of the season, as attention is usually elsewhere, notably Goodwood and York.

The only horse I noted in the race was POWER BENDER. The 10f on the July Course is not quite as stiff a test as across the flat on the Rowley Mile course, but it does produce very reliable results. Up to now he must have been rather an agonising horse for his connections. He had not run as a two year old; and though he had always been there or thereabouts in a series of stakes as a 3 and 4 year old, he was still a maiden. This was rather a moderate field, but he now seemed to have learned something and won with a little to spare. His trainer, Gavin Pritchard-Gordon, is very patient and usually can find something for this type of horse.

11 August Newcastle Northumberland Sprint Trophy (Race 2115: 6f 0–110 3-y.o)

Sometimes horses which have run well at Goodwood are worth following in the Northumberland Sprint Trophy but there was no qualifier this season. It was won well by a filly, CATHERINES WELL with an acceptable *Raceform* speed figure of 69. When a filly begins to improve at this time of the year, it is very difficult for the handicapper to stop her in her tracks.

16 August Ripon The Great St. Wilfrid Handicap (Race 2201: 6f 0–110)

This is one of the best sprint handicaps in the north and often goes to an improving horse. It didn't attract an outstanding field and CATHERINES

WELL carrying a 7lb penalty looked to have a good chance, being +1 in my book. Unfortunately, I was never offered better than 3–1, which did not strike me as good value, so I did not bet. She won again, in splendid style.

20–22 August York
Despite the ideal fast going, I couldn't find any betting opportunities at the 3 day meeting here.

20 August York Wykeham Handicap (Race 2243: 5f 0–100 3-y.o)
I did note MANTON DAN who won the pulling up by 4 lengths in a fast time (*Raceform* speed figure, 89). As a 2 year old, he had won first time out at Goodwood, and then not been disgraced in a competitive Newmarket nursery. He had rather a chequered season so far: aimed rather high in a Newmarket stakes; well beaten in MERDON MELODY's race at Newmarket (Race 441); apparently his stable was then out of form, so he did not reappear until mid-July to win a stakes at Nottingham; and then running well for 5 furlongs, to finish 9th but only 4 lengths behind the winner in the Goodwood Stewards Cup (Race 1898). Clearly he was now going along the right lines.

22 August Newmarket The Buxted Handicap (Race 2293: 6f 0–100 3-y.o)
CATHERINES WELL had an obvious chance, and was marked up at 10–11 accordingly. She was boxed in a furlong out, but as they met the rising ground she found an opening and was soon home and dry. Clearly she was still ahead of the handicapper.

4 September York Hong Kong Marlboro Cup (Race 2485: 6f 0–110)
Although penalised, MANTON DAN appeared to have a good chance in this race. I had to think quite carefully about this. His previous win was over 5f—but as a 2 year old he had won at Goodwood over 6f. The going had to be watched until the last minute—it had been yielding the day before but there was a strong drying wind today and the official forecast was good. He was now running against older horses, but this should be alright at this time of the season.

Of these factors, I was most worried about the going. At the course, the weather was good, and MANTON DAN strode out well on his way to the post.

He won, but only just, at 6–1, much longer odds than I expected. The reader must be wondering by now—even given the reservations, why was MANTON DAN on offer at such a good price?

This race is a good example of how punters can put hope before experience. The favourite at 9–2, PADRE PIO, was in my view quite a good handicapper. Although he had won 3 handicaps, I always had the tantalising feeling that he somehow never seemed quite to run up to his ability. There was no question that he was genuine—I think his problem was that he was neither a 5 furlong nor a 6 furlong horse, but something in between and correspondingly difficult to place.

This season he had struggled on without a realistic hope in the **Great St. Wilfrid** (Race 2201) and was caught on the line in his only other race, at Salisbury at the beginning of June (Race 903). I guessed that many punters fell for the sentimental clichés 'deserves consolation', 'unlucky this season, should go better' 'his turn is near'.

Admittedly something could be said for PADRE PIO, but I could not see the justification for EASTERN SONG being second favourite at 5–1. He had won his last race (Race 2026) at the first August meeting at Brighton, it is true—but that was a £1720 stakes! Not much of a pointer to a £16,600 0–110 handicap at York, I wouldn't have thought.

MANTON DAN only just hung on here, and I reckoned that he had reached his limit.

11 September Salisbury Winterbourne Handicap (Race 2566: 8f 0–90)

The 4 year old FLYHOME won the race with a good display of front running and then quickening at the vital moment.

So far he had had a disappointing season, but perhaps his experiences in 1985 had left him rather perplexed—certainly they perplexed me! He won a 0–75 over 8f at Sandown (Race 631) at the beginning of the season—then at various times ran in apprentice handicaps, an apprentice stakes, an amateurs race, and 0–100 and 0–110 handicaps, over 8f, 10f and 11f 150 yards! If he was tried at a suitable course in his class and distance, he would be worth considering.

11 September Doncaster The Portland Handicap (Race 2577: 5f 140y 0–115)

This is a race of ten won by a well exposed horse which won last time out. FELIPE TORO had won his previous race, at York on 12 July, but in a slow time (45).

He may have been fortunate to win again. For some reason, the starting stalls were not available, and in a badly controlled flag start he stole an irrecoverable few lengths at the beginning, enough to win by 4 lengths, at 11–2.

19 September Ayr The Ayr Gold Cup (Race 2698: 6f 0–115)

The Ayr Western Meeting is the last of the high season meetings. Unusually it was run on fast ground (only 3 out of the previous 12 had been run on good going, and none of those faster than good). It was a very pleasant few days, marred only by the fact that I couldn't find a betting opportunity.

I was saved from a loser by my theories about key races. FELIPE TORO was still well in at −, but records of this race show that the winner of the Portland Handicap rarely wins carrying a penalty—it is better to look for a horse which has run well in this earlier race without winning. There was no such qualifier here, and he was just too late to catch GREEN RUBY, the Stewards Cup winner. The handicapper had now got the measure of MANTON DAN and CATHERINES WELL and they finished 7th and 10th respectively.

20 September Newbury The Autumn Cup (Race 2726: 13f 60y 0–110)

Though outside my distance range this race is usually very competitive and run at a good pace. If it has a contender which has run well in the 14f handicap at the Doncaster St. Leger meeting (in 1985 EASTERN MYSTIC had won here after doing so), then the race is worth considering. This year REVISIT had run in the earlier race but had not been fancied here—he finished a well beaten fifth.

20 September Newbury The Highclere Nursery (Race 2728: 5f £10,222 2-y.o)

This is one of the most valuable nurseries of the season. The winner sometimes runs again in Newmarket nurseries and can then be worth considering. I certainly had high hopes that PRINT would do so—he came away to win by 4 lengths but with in my view about 14 lbs in hand.

It turned out to be a beautiful autumn. Although it was a bit late in the season to look for improving handicappers, the going was nothing to worry about. Even under these ideal conditions, however, I think it best to be extra cautious.

24 September Sandown Wey Handicap (Race 2764: 8f 0–90)

FLYHOME was in at his best distance (8f), and in the same grade as at Salisbury (Race 2566). He had never been asked to do the same thing twice in succession before, but I hoped that this would not be too novel an experience for him. I thought he was level rated with a penalty and he won but only just at 9–2.

I thought this was his limit, but apparently not. After not being able to make all the running in the Cambridgeshire he made all to win a 0–110 handicap over 8f at Ascot. In retrospect, his career seems rather odd and with all due respect to his very capable trainer, I felt he could have been better placed.

3 October Newmarket Unidare Handicap (Race 2878: 10f 0–100 3-y.o)

The going was perfect here, and I selected BILLET in this race. He had won a 0–90 at Leicester on 22 September by galloping on strongly from the distance. Although Leicester is a Class Two course in my book, it does provide a very good test and is similar to Newmarket in some ways.

The winner, MYTENS, is what I call a high-class plodder: he does not have much finishing speed but can set a tremendous gallop. BILLET was struggling with the early pace and was out of it with about 2 furlongs to go. The step up in class had been too much for him at this stage of his career. BILLET proved a popular favourite and was backed down to 5–2: unfortunately I had taken the early 4–1 on offer.

4 October Newmarket Cambridgeshire (Race 2885: 8f 110y 0–110)

I never bet in this race which is usually run over 9f on the Rowley Mile course, this year run over 8f 110y on the July course. It was won well by DALLAS, with POWER BENDER a good second over a distance slightly too short for him.

9 October York Allied Dunbar Handicap (Race 2953: 8f 0–100)

The weather continued fine, and the going fast. The York autumn meeting can be tricky if there is rain about, as the going here can change so quickly. I noted USFAN in this race who won by the narrow margin of ½ length, but definitely with something in hand—just the sort of victory to make the official handicapper perplexed.

11 October York Carling Black Label Lager Handicap (Race 2958: 7f 0–110)

BOOT POLISH accelerated quickly and ran on strongly to win with something in reserve. A winner first time out in a 6f 0–90 at Thirsk (Race 350), he had also won a 0–100 at Pontefract over 6f on 7 July (Race 1467). He had also won twice over 6f as a 3 year old. A typically reliable gelding, he had run some disappointing races over the sprint distance. Tried for the first time here over 7f, he ran on strongly to suggest that this was now his correct distance. Unfortunately he did not run again in 1986.

17 October Newmarket Melbourne Handicap (Race 3060: 8f 0–110)

USFAN appeared to have 1 lb in hand, and was a good bet. I took the 7–2 on offer early, and had a few anxious moments as it took all of Carson's determination to get him into a winning position in the final furlong and keep him there. This was his limit, and I could not see him winning again.

Newmarket 31 October—1 November

The last meeting of the year for us: the fine autumn weather broke and the going was now yielding-soft. Having had a good season I decided to hold off.

SELECTION	RESULT
1153 MOON MADNESS	W 4–1
1330 MANIMSTAR	W 7–2
1493 PATRIACH	W 6–1
1506 AVENTINO	W 4–1
1921 KINGS HEAD	L 7–2
1923 MANIMSTAR	W 6–1
2201 CATHERINES WELL	W 3–1
2485 MANTON DAN	W 6–1
2764 FLYHOME	W 9–2
2878 BILLET	L 4–1
3060 USFAN	W 7–2

11 selections 9 winners 82% winners

Bets—£2950 to a £100 stake
Noted but not backed

412 READY WIT
545 MERDON MELODY
790 SIYAH KALEM
942 FIRST DIVISION
1158 NAVARZATO
1846 ROTHERFIELD GREYS
2958 BOOT POLISH
3026 POWER BENDER

CHAPTER ELEVEN
Summary

Chapter One Why Handicaps?
Form works out better in handicaps than in any other type of race. Therefore you should only bet on handicaps.
Never follow non-handicap form into a handicap.
Be selective—concentrate on the better class handicaps, ie 0–90 and above.
Only back a horse to do what it has done before.
Learn to read races and draw your own conclusions.

Chapters Two and Three How Handicaps are Compiled; Compiling a Private Handicap
Always look carefully at horses carrying penalties—there may be a good opportunity for a bet here.
Never bet in selling handicaps, apprentice handicaps or nurseries.
Good going usually provides the most reliable form.

Chapter Four The Art of Race Reading
Favour courses with an uphill finish when you are learning to race-read: the results are much more clear-cut.
Choose a good pair of binoculars, and try to note the position of the first six finishers—even if your selection is well down the field.
Remember: pace makes the race.
Always look for a horse which is able to produce a strong late finish.
Be patient and alert—sometimes you may have to wait quite a while before you see the kind of horse which can win again.

Chapter Five How to Use a Private Handicap
A horse can give away weight but not distance. Carrying less weight will not make a horse run any faster, although having more weight may slow him down.
Look for a horse with good recent form—that is, within the last 28 days.
Geldings are the most reliable and consistent type of horse.
Instead of looking for 'a winner in this race', look for 'a race for this winner'.
Make your selection before you go to the course. At the course, only change your mind about your selection on the basis of what you have seen, and not because of the betting market.
Go by yourself, unless you can find someone else who shares your serious approach to racing.

Chapter Six Key Races
Remember not only the old saying 'Horses for Courses'—but 'Horses for Races': year after year, some key races are won by a horse with a particular kind of form.

Chapter Seven Jockeys and Trainers
Look for a good apprentice jockey, claiming 5lbs or 7lbs.

Chapter Eight Betting to Win
Record all bets.
Bet on the course (no tax).
Remember: profit for the season, and not profit for the day.
Wait until everything is in your favour.
Never ever bet odds on.
Never bet less than 7–2.
Learn from your mistakes.
Maximise your winnings—don't chase your losses.
Choose a sensible staking system: either straight win bets at a fixed amount, or, 10% of your bank.

Chapter Nine Racing Through the Season
Only bet from the Epsom Derby meeting (first week of June) to the Ayr Western meeting (third week of September).

RACEFORM BOOKS

Spring 1990

RACEFORM 1989 FLAT ANNUAL. All last season's form
on the Flat with comments on running.
The Jockey Club's Official Record £19.00

HORSES IN TRAINING 1990. 15,000 Flat and
N.H. horses with their breeding and owner's name listed
under 700 trainers £10.50

TIMECHECK '89. All Speed Figures of 30 and
above achieved last Flat, showing where, when, at what distance
and on what going £8.95

100 WINNERS FOR 1990. Pen portraits by Raceform experts
on horses likely to do particularly well during
the coming Flat season £2.95

HOW TO WIN AT HANDICAP RACING by Patrick
Kilgallon £4.95

GREYHOUND RACING FOR PROFIT by Mark Sealey £2.95

HOW TO FIND VALUE WHEN BETTING by Malcolm
Howard £4.95

CHASEFORM ANNUAL 1988-89. All last season's N.H. form
with comments on how they ran and jumped £17.00

All prices including postage and packing
Remit with order to
RACEFORM LTD.
COMPTON, NEWBURY, BERKSHIRE RG16 0NL
Access and Visa cardholders can order by telephone
at any time on 0635 578080